Renate Seebauer
NACHHILFE ENGLISCH
OBERSTUFE 2

Renate Seebauer

Nachhilfe Englisch Oberstufe 2

Regeln
Übungen
Lösungen

Verlag Leitner · Wien

CIP-Kurztitelaufnahme der Deutschen Bibliothek

Seebauer, Renate:
Nachhilfe Englisch/Renate Seebauer. –
Wien: Leitner
(Leitners Studienhelfer)

Oberstufe:
2 (1987)
ISBN 3-85157-055-3

© by Verlag Leitner 1987
in Herold Druck- und Verlagsgesellschaft m. b. H., Wien
Illustrationen: Marianne Reindl
Druck: Herold, Wien 8

ISBN 3-85157-055-3

INHALTSVERZEICHNIS

Vorwort 9

THE ARTICLE – DER ARTIKEL 12

1. INDEFINITE ARTICLE – UNBESTIMMTER ARTIKEL 12
2. DEFINITE ARTICLE – BESTIMMTER ARTIKEL 18

Übungen 26

THE NOUN – DAS HAUPTWORT (SUBSTANTIV) 30

1. GENDER AND PLURAL – GESCHLECHT UND MEHRZAHLBILDUNG 30
2. "COMMON CASE" AND "POSSESSIVE CASE" 46

Übungen 52

THE PRONOUNS – DIE FÜRWÖRTER (PRONOMINA) 56

1. PERSONAL PRONOUNS – DIE PERSÖNLICHEN FÜRWÖRTER (PERSONALPRONOMINA) 56
2. POSSESSIVE PRONOUNS – DIE BESITZANZEIGENDEN FÜRWÖRTER (POSSESSIVPRONOMINA) 62
3. REFLEXIVE PRONOUNS – DIE RÜCKBEZÜGLICHEN FÜRWÖRTER (REFLEXIVPRONOMINA) 66
4. RECIPROCAL PRONOUNS – DIE PRONOMINA DER GEGENSEITIGKEIT (REZIPROKE PRONOMINA) 70

5. DEMONSTRATIVE PRONOUNS –
   DIE HINWEISENDEN FÜRWÖRTER
   (DEMONSTRATIVPRONOMINA) 70

6. INTERROGATIVE PRONOUNS –
   DIE FRAGEFÜRWÖRTER
   (INTERROGATIVPRONOMINA) 74

7. RELATIVE PRONOUNS –
   DIE BEZÜGLICHEN FÜRWÖRTER
   (RELATIVPRONOMINA) 78

8. INDEFINITE PRONOUNS –
   DIE UNBESTIMMTEN FÜRWÖRTER
   (INDEFINITPRONOMINA) 82
   Some – Any 83
   Every – Each (of) – Any 85
   All – Whole 87
   Both – The Two – Either – Neither 89
   One – Other – Another 91
   No – None – No one – Nobody – Nothing 91
   Much – Many – Little – Few 95

Übungen 96

**THE ADJECTIVE – DAS EIGENSCHAFTSWORT
(ADJEKTIV)** 108

1. COMPARISON AND USE – STEIGERUNG
   UND ANWENDUNG 108

2. PARTICULAR ADJECTIVES – BESONDER-
   HEITEN EINZELNER ADJEKTIVA 122
   Adjektiva mit Präpositionen 123
   Breit, weit 125
   Dumm 125
   Ernst 127
   Fremd 127
   Gescheit 127
   Groß 129
   Gut 131
   Klein 133

Leicht	135
Lustig	135
Schlecht	135
Schön	137
Schwer	139
Übungen	140

THE ADVERB – DAS UMSTANDSWORT (ADVERB) 148

Übungen 156

THE PREPOSITIONS – DIE VORWÖRTER (PRÄPOSITIONEN) 160

1. POSITION OF PREPOSITIONS – DIE STELLUNG DER PRÄPOSITIONEN 161

2. USE OF PARTICULAR PREPOSITIONS – GEBRAUCH EINZELNER PRÄPOSITIONEN 161

An / am	161
Auf	163
Aus	163
Außer	165
Außen	167
Bei	167
Bis	167
Durch	169
Gegen	169
Gegenüber	171
Hinauf	171
Hinunter	171
Hinter	173
In / im	173
Längs / entlang	175
Mit	175
Nach	175
Nahe	177
Neben	177

Ohne 177
Seit 177
Trotz 179
Über 179
Um 181
Unter 181
Von 183
Vor 183
Während 185
Wegen 185
Zu 185
Zwischen 187

3. VERBEN MIT UNTERSCHIEDLICHEN PRÄPOSITIONEN 188

Übungen 192

THE NUMERALS – DIE ZAHLWÖRTER (NUMERALE) 202

1. CARDINAL NUMBERS – GRUNDZAHLEN (KARDINALZAHLEN) 202

2. ORDINAL NUMBERS – ORDNUNGSZAHLEN (ORDINALZAHLEN) 204

3. MULTIPLYING NUMBERS – WIEDERHOLUNGS- UND VERVIELFÄLTIGUNGSZAHLEN 206

4. FRACTIONAL NUMBERS, FUNDAMENTAL RULES OF ARITHMETIC – BRUCHZAHLEN, GRUNDRECHNUNGSARTEN 206

Übungen 208

Lösungen der Übungsaufgaben 209
Stichwortverzeichnis 231

VORWORT

Das vorliegende Übungsbuch „NACHHILFE ENGLISCH, Oberstufe 2" versteht sich als Fortführung der bewährten Handreichungen für die Unterstufe sowie als Fortsetzung des 1. Bandes.
„NACHHILFE ENGLISCH, Oberstufe 2" wurde speziell für Schüler ab der 9. Schulstufe konzipiert.
Die Einsatzmöglichkeiten dieses Bandes gestalten sich mannigfaltig. Durch den Erwerb grammatikalischer Regeln und Grundstrukturen erlangt der Lernende Sicherheit im richtigen Sprachgebrauch, sowohl in der mündlichen als auch in der schriftlichen Anwendung. Die übersichtliche Art der Darstellung – links die Musterbeispiele, rechts im Kästchen die Regel – die sich im Band „GRAMMATIKTRAINING ENGLISCH" bestens bewährt hat, wurde auch hier beibehalten.
Da der richtige Gebrauch des Eigenschaftsworts beim Abfassen von Aufsätzen immer wieder Schwierigkeiten bereitet, wurde der Abschnitt über die „Besonderheiten einzelner Adjektiva" so ausführlich gestaltet. Die intensive Auseinandersetzung mit dem Abschnitt „Gebrauch einzelner Präpositionen" soll besonders dazu beitragen, „Germanismen" zu beseitigen. In allen Abschnitten wurde großer Wert auf gebräuchliche englische Redewendungen gelegt, deren Integration in den aktiven Sprachgebrauch vor allem eine Hilfe für den Verfasser von Nacherzählungen und Aufsätzen bieten soll.
Die Durchführung der Übungsaufgaben (mündlich und / oder schriftlich) sowie die durch die Lösungen gegebene Möglichkeit der unmittelbaren Kontrolle garantiert die Festigung grammatischer Gesetzmäßigkeiten. 108 gezielte Übungen mit insgesamt fast 900 Übungssätzen ermöglichen die Umsetzung des Regelwissens in den aktiven Sprachgebrauch.

Viel Freude und Erfolg beim Erwerb der Fremdsprache wünscht
              Die Autorin

REGELN UND ÜBUNGEN

THE ARTICLE

INDEFINITE ARTICLE

In a word, I missed the bus.

He'll be back **in a month or two**.

Tom and his cousin are **of an age**.

The patients were examined **one at a time**.

	not stressed	stressed
a boy	[ə]	[ei]
an Austrian boy	[ən]	[æn]

a room, a book, a man, a woman ...

a uniform [ə'ju:nifɔ:m]

a university, a one-year-old baby

an apple, an English boy, an interesting story, an opera, ...

an ugly witch, ...

an hour [ən'auə]

an M. P. [ən'em'pi:]

 Übung 1

DER ARTIKEL

1. UNBESTIMMTER ARTIKEL

Der **unbestimmte Artikel** „a / an" ist aus dem **Zahlwort** „one" hervorgegangen.

Sein ursprünglicher Charakter als **Zahlwort** ist noch in einigen Redewendungen erhalten.

in a word	mit einem Wort
in a month or two	in ein, zwei Monaten
in a day	in einem Tag
of an age	gleichaltrig
one at a time	einer nach dem anderen

Der **unbestimmte Artikel** lautet im Englischen für alle drei Geschlechter und für alle Fälle „a" bzw. „an".

Beachte die Aussprache!

– a: vor konsonantischem Anlaut

Achtung! Es kommt nicht auf die Schreibweise an, sondern auf die Aussprache!

– an: vor vokalischem Anlaut

Achtung! Es kommt nicht auf die Schreibweise an, sondern auf die Aussprache!

My friend wants to become a teacher.
Mr Brown is a scientist.
That man is a baron, he is the Baron of Blackworth.

Mr Dupont is a Frenchman.
Rita is an Italian girl.
He is a negro.
Green Feather is a Red Indian.

Mr Smith is a Roman Catholic, his wife is a Protestant.

Mr Blackwell earns £ 2 an hour.
An apple a day keeps the doctor away.
The apples are 80 pence a pound.

These curtains sell at 5 £ a metre.
This juice is 75 pence a bottle.
The farmer sells the plums at 60 pence a box.

He is known as a good playwright.
The trunk of a tree served us for a table.

The Millers found such a nice restaurant.
Many a student, who started at the University, failed.
What a splendid idea!
Mary is rather a clever girl.
It was quite an easy test.
They returned half an hour later.

Gebrauch:
Der **unbestimmte Artikel** ordnet das einzelne in eine Gruppe ein, drückt die Zugehörigkeit zu einer Gruppe aus.

Der **unbestimmte Artikel** steht

- zur Angabe des **Berufes, Standes,** ... nach Verben wie „to be, to become, to remain, to live, to return ..."

- zur Angabe der **Nationalität, Rasse**

- zur Angabe der **Religion**, der **politischen Zugehörigkeit**

- bei **Zeit-, Gewichts- und Maßeinheiten**

- zur Bezeichnung der **Mengeneinheit**

- nach as und for

Beachte die Stellung des unbestimmten Artikels **nach:**

such a	solch ein
many a	mancher
what a	was für ein ...!
rather a	ziemlich (sehr)
quite a	ganz
half a	halb

He was elected **mayor of Vienna**.
Mr Hoover is **headmaster of Greenwood College**.

When he moved to Austria he <u>turned</u> **Roman Catholic**.

She got the title <u>of</u> **doctor**.

The children had <u>plenty of</u> **time**.

All the people were **in a hurry**.

When he realized that he had forgotten the flowers he was quite **at a loss**.

What **a pity**! He had **a sore throat**, so he could only speak **in a low voice**.

They appreciated her excellent behaviour **in a high degree**.

Take a seat, please.

As a rule he arrives at 8.15.

 *Übungen 2, 3*

Beachte!

Der unbestimmte Artikel steht NICHT

- wenn nur <u>eine</u> Person zur selben Zeit einen Rang oder Titel innehaben kann
- nach „to turn" (werden)
- nach Berufsbezeichnungen, wenn eine Beifügung mit „of" folgt
- vor <u>plenty of</u> (eine Menge) und (meistens nicht) vor <u>part of</u> (ein Teil)

Beachte die idiomatischen Wendungen!

to be in a hurry	in Eile sein
to be at a loss	in Verlegenheit sein
it's a pity	es ist schade, wie schade
to have a cough (a headache, a sore throat, ...)	Husten (Kopfweh, Halsweh, ...) haben
in a loud/low voice	mit lauter/leiser Stimme
in a high degree	in hohem Maße
to take a seat	Platz nehmen
as a rule	in der Regel
all of a sudden	plötzlich
to be in a temper	zornig sein

DEFINITE ARTICLE

the tree, the man, the boy, the children, ...
the university [ðə juːniˈvəsiti]

the English lesson, the apples, the orange ...
the hour ...

She is <u>the</u> woman for this job.

 *Übung 4*

The man we met yesterday was Bill's uncle.
Attention! **The stairs** are slippery.
When **the cat** is away, **the mice** will play.

The Hoovers moved to London.
The Kennedys came over from Ireland.

I've seen both, **the Highlands** and **the Lowlands**.
The Bermudas are famous for their climate.

The Großglockner is Austria's highest mountain.
Mr Edward Whimper was the first man to climb **the Matterhorn**.

Brighton lies in **the south**, Edinburgh in **the north**.

2. BESTIMMTER ARTIKEL

Der **bestimmte** Artikel „the" ist aus dem **hinweisenden Fürwort** „this / that" hervorgegangen.

Der **bestimmte** Artikel „**the**" hat für alle Geschlechter und für alle Fälle der Einzahl und Mehrzahl nur eine Form.

Beachte die Aussprache!

– [ðə]: vor Wörtern mit konsonantischem Anlaut

Achtung! Es kommt nicht auf die Schreibweise an, sondern auf die Aussprache!

– [ði]: vor Wörtern mit vokalischem Anlaut (oft auch h)

– [ði:]: mit stark hinweisendem Charakter

Gebrauch:

Der **bestimmte Artikel** hebt das einzelne aus einer gleichartigen Gruppe heraus.

Der **bestimmte Artikel** steht

– bei **Familiennamen im Plural**

– bei **geographischen Bezeichnungen im Plural**

– bei den **Namen nichtenglischer Berge**

– bei den **Himmelsrichtungen**

They crossed the United States from east to west.

He was kept prisoner in **the Tower of London**.
The first district of Vienna is also called **the City**.

<u>In</u> **the evening** he used to eat cornflakes.
<u>On</u> **the morning** of January 1st they got up later than usual.
<u>During</u> **the afternoon** the ladies had a friendly chat.

It's possible to earn <u>double</u> **the money** in <u>half</u> **the time**.
<u>Both</u> (the) girls were very diligent.

All the boys of the sixth form played football.
All boys like sports.

Not only the boys, but also the girls had to study hard.

That was the first and the last time I met him.

Mr Brown is a teacher.
Ann and **Nelly** are twins.
Captain Greene is a police officer.
Lord Nelson won the Battle of Trafalgar.
Old Mr Brown had to stay at home.
Poor Nelly didn't get any presents.

Beachte die Redewendung:

from north to south
from east to west

- bei Gattungsnamen in der Verwendung als Eigennamen

- bei **Tageszeiten** in Verbindung mit Präpositionen (in, on, during ...)

Beachte die Stellung des bestimmten Artikels **nach:**

half, double, (both)

Achtung! all
- mit Artikel (alle aus einer bestimmten Gruppe)
- ohne Artikel („alle": verallgemeinernd)

Beachte die Wiederholung des bestimmten Artikels:

- zur Hervorhebung oder Gegenüberstellung einzelner Personen, Dinge

- wenn mehrere Adjektive unterschiedlicher Bedeutung vor einem Hauptwort in der Einzahl stehen

Beachte!
Der bestimmte Artikel steht NICHT

- bei **Eigennamen** jeder Art (bei Personennamen und Bezeichnungen der Familienmitglieder)
  - bei **Personennamen in Verbindung mit** vorangehenden **Titel-, Berufs- und Verwandtschaftsbezeichnungen**
  - bei **Personennamen in Verbindung mit gefühlsbetonten Adjektiven** wie „young, old, little, big, poor ..."

He left **America** and found a new home in **Austria**.
Paris is the capital of **France**.
Ben Nevis is a snow-capped mountain.
Many Londoners spend their holidays in **Sicily**.

Mount Everest, Cape Horn, Lake Ontario, ...

There is a nice fountain in the Lake <u>of</u> Geneva.

Continental Europe
Southern Europe
Ancient Rome
Medieval Vienna

Fleet Street, Edgeware Road, Trafalgar Square, Hyde Park, ...
Tower Bridge, Westminster Abbey, ...

We'll travel to Edinburgh **in spring**.
They'll be back **in June**.
He arrived **on Monday**.

Joe will arrive <u>at</u> midday.

Time is money.
Such is **life**.
"**Love** is a many splendored thing" is the title of a famous song.

School is over at four. <u>(Unterricht)</u>
They went to **church** at 9. <u>(Gottesdienst)</u>
He was at **table**. <u>(beim Essen)</u>

Woman is the helpmate of **man**.

Coal is mined in Newcastle.
Gold is very expensive.
This costume is made of **wool**.

- bei **geographischen Eigennamen** (Erdteile, Länder, Städte, englische Berge, Inseln, ...)

● bei Namen von Bergen, Seen, ..., wenn „Mount, Cape, Lake, ..." vorangehen

Beachte den **bestimmten Artikel,** wenn der Eigenname mit „of" angefügt ist.

● bei Länder- und Städtenamen in Verbindung mit Adjektiven

continental, southern, northern, east, west, central, modern, ancient, medieval, ...

● vor Bezeichnungen für Straßen, Plätze, Parks, Brücken, Gebäude, ...

- bei **Zeitbestimmungen** (Jahreszeiten, Monate, Wochentage, Fest- und Feiertage, ...)

● bei Tageszeiten in Verbindung mit „at"

- bei **Abstrakta** wie

time, life, love, art, fortune, poverty, nature, hatred, fate, hunger, simplicity, virtue, ...

● bei „school, university, church, prison, bed, table, ...", wenn sie im allgemeinen Sinn gebraucht werden

● bei „man, woman, ..." im allgemeinen Sinn

- bei **Stoffnamen** wie „coal, iron, stone, water, gold, cotton, blood, wool, ..."

English literature is famous all over the world.
Mr White is experienced in **foreign policy**.
I don't like **modern art**.

Boys will be **boys**.
Cats like **fish**.

Heaven will help you.
Go to **Hell**!

Most **children** like sweets.
Most **people** buy Christmas presents for their friends.

Study this text **from the beginning.**

The boys failed **with the exception of** Jimmy.
Little Tommy could solve the puzzle **with the help of** Dad.

It is the fashion to wear a mini-skirt.

He recognized her **at first sight.**
The Coopers live in the country, the Blackwells live **in town.**

In case of emergency, pull here!

He can't help you now, he is **at work.**

Let's **shake hands.**

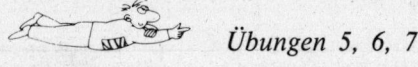 *Übungen 5, 6, 7*

- bei **Abstrakta** und **Stoffnamen in Verbindung mit Adjektiven** wie „English, foreign, domestic, natural, human, private, public, modern, ..."

- bei **Gattungsnamen im Plural** wie „boys, children, cats, dogs, ..."

- vor **religiösen Begriffen** wie „Paradise, Heaven, Hell ..."

- vor „most" in der Bedeutung „die meisten"

Beachte die idiomatischen Wendungen!

- MIT bestimmtem Artikel

from the beginning	vom Anfang an
in the presence of	in Gegenwart von
with the exception of	mit Ausnahme von
with the help of	mit Hilfe von
it is the custom	es ist Brauch
it is the fashion	es ist Mode

- OHNE bestimmten Artikel

to go by train (bus, car, ...)	mit dem Zug (Bus, Auto, ...) fahren
at first sight	auf den ersten Blick
to live in town	in der Stadt wohnen
in fact	in der Tat
in case of	im Falle von
in practice	in der Praxis
to be at hand	bei der Hand sein
to be at work	bei (an) der Arbeit sein
to set sail	die Segel hissen
to shake hands	sich die Hand geben

ÜBUNGEN

1. Jedem Wort (jeder Wortgruppe) soll der „unbestimmte Artikel" vorangestellt werden!

... man, ... Englishman, ... Italian, ... university, ... one-year-old girl, ... home, ... Member of Parliament, ... Austrian flag, ... M. P., ... house, ... hour, ... huge building, ... ugly wizard, ... American car, ... red apple, ... orange, ... uniform, ... interesting musical, ... opera.

2. Folgende Sätze sollen sinngemäß übersetzt werden!

a) Tom möchte Arzt werden.

b) Nur ein Bub aus Freds Klasse wurde Mechaniker.

c) Ist Herr Dupont Franzose? – Nein, er ist Italiener.

d) Schau, Pat hat sich als Indianer verkleidet.

e) Er war als ausgezeichneter Schauspieler bekannt.

f) Sie verdiente 120 £ pro Woche.

g) Die Vorhänge wurden um 3 £ pro Meter verkauft.

h) Der Professor prüfte einen nach dem anderen.

i) Der Autor wird das Buch in ein, zwei Wochen fertig haben.

j) So manches Mädchen, das eine Sekretärin werden will, wird nur eine Schreibkraft.

k) Was für einen modernen Haarschnitt du hast!

l) Hat euch der Film gefallen? Ja, es war ein ganz amüsanter Film.

m) Tom ist viel größer, obwohl Tom und sein Cousin gleich alt sind.

n) Er wird in einer halben Stunde zurück sein.

o) Ein großer Stein diente uns als Tisch.

3. „Unbestimmter Artikel" oder „kein Artikel"?

a) Mr Hoover was ... Protestant. When he moved to Italy he turned ... Roman Catholic.
b) Jim wants to become ... teacher. His father is ... headmaster of Trinity College.
c) All the people were ... hurry.
d) The teacher spoke in ... loud voice.
e) Take ... seat, please.
f) Mr Brown was ... Captain of the "Sunflower".
g) Now he is ... mechanic.
h) After working as ... guide, she turned ... journalist.
i) Mrs Brown was in ... temper when Bob arrived late.
j) I have ... cough and ... sore throat, and I'm sure I have ... temperature, too.
k) The student was quite at ... loss when the professor asked him a simple question.
l) He was elected ... Lord Mayor of London.

4. Es soll jeweils die richtige Aussprache angekreuzt werden!

	[ðə]	[ði]				[ðə]	[ði]	
a)			the apple		f)			the amusing film
b)			the English children		g)			the uniform
c)			the right job		h)			the high mountain
d)			the university		i)			the hour
e)			the ugly witch		j)			the Austrian State Treaty

5. Folgende Sätze sollen sinngemäß übersetzt werden!

a) Sie durchquerten Österreich von West nach Ost.
b) Kärnten liegt im Süden, Niederösterreich im Norden.
c) Am Abend gingen sie gewöhnlich spazieren.
d) Es ist unmöglich, das doppelte Geld in der halben Zeit zu verdienen.
e) Das mittelalterliche Wien ist sehenswert.

f) Alle Schüler unseres Colleges kamen zur Party.

g) Alle Mädchen tanzen gern, alle Buben essen gern.

h) Nicht nur die Schüler, sondern auch die Lehrer nahmen an diesem Theaterstück teil.

i) Sie werden im Frühjahr nach Spanien reisen.

j) Im antiken Rom gab es viele Tempel.

k) Viele Könige sind in der Westminster Abtei begraben.

l) Die Tower-Brücke ist eine Zugbrücke.

m) Die amerikanische Literatur ist in ganz Europa bekannt.

n) Der Unterricht beginnt im September.

o) Der Himmel wird dir helfen.

p) Die meisten Leute machen einmal im Jahr Urlaub.

6. *Der vollständige Satz soll auf Englisch wiedergegeben werden!*

a) You should read this book _____.
   (vom Anfang an)

b) He was given the prize _____ the Queen.
   (in Gegenwart von)

c) She was attracted by his good looks _____.
   (auf den ersten Blick)

d) Dad can't play with you now, he is _____.
   (bei der Arbeit)

e) That's theory, but it's quite different _____.
   (in der Praxis)

f) They were saved _____ a helicopter.
   (mit Hilfe von)

g) There was no petrol in the tank, so they went _____.
   (mit dem Bus)

h) There's a gentle breeze today, let's _____.
   (die Segel hissen)

i) All the girls came to the party _____ Ann.
   (mit Ausnahme von)

j) In England it's _____ to wear a school uniform.
   (der Brauch)

k) As the tools were _____ he repaired the lawn-mower.
   (bei der Hand)

l) _____ emergency, press this button.
   (Im Falle von)

7. „Unbestimmter Artikel", „bestimmter Artikel" oder „kein Artikel"?

a) Such is ... life.

b) On ... morning of December 25th the children were excited.

c) Last summer Mr Smith climbed ... Dachstein and ... Ben Nevis.

d) When he met her unexpectedly he was quite at ... loss.

e) It's ... pity you can't watch TV this evening.

f) ... school is over at two.

g) ... Fleet Street is the street of newspapers.

h) Mr Brown is known as ... excellent scientist.

i) Mr Blackwell is ... cashier at the Bank of England.

j) Mr Visconti is ... Italian.

k) ... old Mr Jones is experienced in languages.

l) Bregenz lies in ... west.

THE NOUN

GENDER AND PLURAL

What is the **boy** doing? – **He** is studying French.
Why is **Nelly** late? – **She** missed the bus.
Where is the **newspaper**? – **It's** on the table over there.

The **doctor** couldn't come. ⟨ **He** was in hospital.
She was too busy.

The **pupil** had to study hard. ⟨ **He** was very diligent.
She took her exams yesterday.

Most of the **male students** took their doctor's degree.
She went to the cinema with her **boy-friend**.
Most of Jim's teachers are **lady-teachers**.

The **actor** was very good, the **actress** was excellent.
Tom acted the **hero**, Mary acted the **heroine**.

DAS HAUPTWORT (SUBSTANTIV)

1. GESCHLECHT UND MEHRZAHLBILDUNG

Im Englischen ist das **Geschlecht des Substantivs** im allgemeinen nicht an der Form erkennbar.

Das **grammatische Geschlecht** wird durch das **natürliche Geschlecht** bestimmt.

Bezeichnung des Geschlechts

– bei **Personen**

- Viele Berufsbezeichnungen gelten für beide Geschlechter

cook	Koch, Köchin
driver	Fahrer, Fahrerin
singer	Sänger, Sängerin
shop-assistant	Verkäufer, Verkäuferin
student	Student, Studentin
teacher	Lehrer, Lehrerin
writer	Schriftsteller, Schriftstellerin

Das natürliche Geschlecht wird ausgedrückt durch

- he / his, she / her
- Voranstellen von **man, woman (lady)**

  boy, girl

  male, female

- Das Geschlecht ist durch **Endungen** gekennzeichnet: -ess, -ine

master	– mistress	Meister(in)
steward	– stewardess	Steward(eß)
host	– hostess	Gastgeber(in)

Prince Charles and **Princess** Diana opened the fair.

man	– woman	father	– mother
son	– daughter	uncle	– aunt
brother	– sister	king	– queen

At the last race, a **horse** broke **its** neck.

Have you got a **he-cat** or a **she-cat**?

The **female fox** is very dangerous.

Look! The **hen-robin** is flying to her nest.

dog	– bitch	gander	– goose
bull (ox)	– cow	lion	– lioness
drake	– duck	tiger	– tigress

The **Rhinoceros** took off **his** skin.

Look, **Pussy** is coming! **She**'s caught a mouse.

Where's my **handbag**? I can't find **it**.

They saw the Großglockner and **his** glaciers.

The **sun** is high up in the sky shining in all **his** glory.

duke	–	duchess	Herzog(in)
prince	–	princess	Prinz(essin)
hero	–	heroine	Held(in)

- ● Das natürliche Geschlecht ist durch unterschiedliche Vokabeln gegeben

– bei **Tieren**

- ● Bezeichnungen für Tiere sind im allgemeinen sächlich
- ● Viele Bezeichnungen für Tiere gelten für beide Geschlechter: wolf, cat, robin, ...

Das natürliche Geschlecht wird ausgedrückt durch Voranstellen von

- ● he / she
- ● male / female
- ● cock / hen (bei Vögeln)
- ● Das natürliche Geschlecht ist durch unterschiedliche Vokabeln gegeben

- ● In Tiergeschichten oder bei Haustieren wird die personifizierte Form „he / she" verwendet

– bei **Dingen, Sachen**

- ● im allgemeinen sächlich

Beachte!

Personifiziert werden gebraucht

- ● männlich: Namen von Bergen, Flüssen, ...
  the sun (vgl. sol-is, le soleil)

The children learned about **Britain** and **her** people.

The Titanic sank on **her** first voyage.

"What's the matter with our **plane**?" **She**'s losing height.

"Fill **her** up, please!" he said. (volltanken)

Übungen 8, 9

book	– books	[s]
boy	– boys	[z]
box	– boxes	[iz]

bush	– bushes	[iz]
page	– pages	[iz]
hobby	– hobbies	
family	– families	
boy	– boys	
journey	– journeys	

The **Kennedys** came over from Ireland.
There are two **Nellys** in our class.

potato	– potatoes
tomato	– tomatoes
photo	– photos
dynamo	– dynamos
trio	– trios

● weiblich: Länder,
Schiffe, Flugzeuge, Lokomotiven, Autos, ...

the moon, vor allem poetisch
(vgl. luna-ae, **la** lune)

Im Englischen wird die **Mehrzahl (der Plural)** des Substantivs im allgemeinen durch Anfügen eines „-s" gebildet.

Die Aussprache erfolgt

stimmlos

stimmhaft

silbisch (nach Zischlauten)

Beachte die Schreib- und Ausspracheregeln!

– Endung **-es** nach Zischlaut

– **-y** wird nach einem Konsonant zu **-ie**

– **-y bleibt** nach Vokalen und in Eigennamen

– **-o** wird in der Mehrzahl zu **-oes**

– **-os** steht bei jenen Substantiven in der Mehrzahl, die noch als Fremdwörter empfunden werden

calf	– calves	loaf	– loaves
knife	– knives	wolf	– wolves
leaf	– leaves	-self	– -selves
chief	– chiefs	proof	– proofs
roof	– roofs	safe	– safes

bath	– baths	[ðz]
path	– paths	[ðz]
cloth	– cloths	[θs]

man	– men	goose	– geese
woman	– women	mouse	– mice
foot	– feet	louse	– lice

There were five **oxen** in the cowshed.

Five **children** were playing in the park.

Put three **pennies** into the slot.

You can buy a bar of chocolate for 10 **pence**.

These **cloths** are good for cleaning the windows.

Take these **clothes** to the cleaner's.

- Wörter **germanischer Herkunft** auf **-f, -fe** bilden den Plural auf **-ves** [vz]

- Wörter **romanischer Herkunft** auf **-f, -fe, -oof** bilden den Plural auf **-f(e)s** [fs]

Achtung!

Der **stimmlose Konsonant** [θ] am Wortende ist im Plural

- stimmhaft [ð] nach langem Vokal

- stimmlos [θ] nach kurzem Vokal

Besonderheiten in der Mehrzahlbildung:

- Einige Substantive bilden den Plural mit **Umlaut**

- Mehrzahlbildung durch Anhängen von **-en, -ren** bei ox – oxen, child – children

- Substantive mit 2 Pluralformen unterschiedlicher Bedeutung

penny ⟨ pennies (einzelne Münzen)
        pence (Preisangabe)

cloth ⟨ cloths (Tücher)
        clothes (Kleidung, Kleidungsstücke)

bacillus – bacilli   analysis – analyses
terminus – termini   crisis   – crises
datum   – data
medium – media

appendix – appendices, appendixes
index   – indices, indexes

dogma   – dogmas
asylum – asylums

girl-**friends**   **lookers**-on
brothers-in-law   **passers**-by
apple-**trees**   boy **scouts**

ten-year-**olds**   stay-at-**homes** (Stubenhocker)
merry-go-**rounds**   close-**ups** (Nahaufnahmen)

She drank two **mouthfuls** of juice and ran out.
A recipe: Take three **spoonfuls** of milk ...

Übungen 10, 11

There were twenty **sheep** in the meadow.
The hunter could only see a few **deer**.

Six **aircraft** landed within the last five minutes.

He caught many **fish**.

five **dozen** eggs, three **hundred** spectators, forty **thousand** inhabitants, ...

- Fremdwörter behalten oft die Pluralform der Herkunftssprache
  - lateinische, griechische Endung

  - lateinische oder englische Endung

  - englische Endung

- Zusammengesetzte Substantive
  - das **Grundwort** enthält die Pluralendung

  - das **letzte Wort** erhält die Pluralendung, wenn kein Bestandteil des Wortes der eigentliche Sinnträger ist
  - Wörter auf „-ful" haben das Pluralzeichen am Wortende: handful, cupful, plateful, ...

Gebrauch von Singular und Plural:

- **Substantive mit gleicher Form für Singular und Plural**
  - in der Form der Einzahl stehen

    sheep, deer

    craft (aircraft, hovercraft, ...)

    fish – fishes (Fischarten ... wird immer seltener gebraucht)

    dozen, hundred, thousand, million, ... erhalten kein Plural-s in Verbindung mit einem Zahlwort

dozens of eggs, **hundreds** of spectators, many **thousands** of inhabitants, ...

That's just the right **means** of transport.
"Dallas" is a very popular **series** of films.

The dog wanted some **water**.
Rabbits like **grass**.

Mathematics is an interesting subject.
Acoustics deals with sounds.

Measles is a serious illness, so is **chickenpox**.

Dominoes is one of my favourite games.

"There's no **business** like show business" is the title of a famous song.
All the **furniture** in Tom's room is built-in.
This **homework** was very easy.
The children are making good **progress**.
This was good **news**.
Her **knowledge** of English is excellent.

The **surroundings** of Vienna are very nice.

Beachte!

Ohne Zahlwort und **nach MANY** steht die Pluralform!

- in der Form der Mehrzahl (Endung auf -s) stehen means, series, gallows, headquarters, barracks, ...

– **Substantive, die im Englischen immer im Singular stehen**
  - Stoffnamen
  - Namen von Wissenschaften mit der Endung „**-ics**": athletics, mechanics, politics, optics, physics, statistics, ...
  - Namen von Krankheiten
  - Namen von Spielen
  - folgende Substantive, die im Deutschen in der Einzahl u n d Mehrzahl gebraucht werden

advice	Rat, Ratschläge
business	Geschäft, Geschäfte
furniture	Möbel, Möbelstücke
homework	Hausübung, Aufgaben
information	Information, Informationen
equipment	Ausrüstung, Ausrüstungsgegenstände
progress	Fortschritt, Fortschritte
strength	Kraft, Stärke
news	Neuigkeit, Neuigkeiten
knowledge	Wissen

– **Substantive, die immer im Plural stehen**
  - Begriffe, die einzelne Teile zu einem Ganzen zusammenfassen

arms	Waffen
belongings	Habe
stairs	Treppe

Richard the Lionhearted ruled England during the **Middle Ages**.
Attention! The **stairs** are very slippery.
His **riches** do not make him happy.

Where are your **trousers**, Tom?
These **scissors** are very dangerous.
Little boys should go to bed now – put on your **pyjamas**.
Don't forget your **goggles** when you go skiing.

I need <u>some</u> **scissors**.
I want <u>a pair of</u> red **pyjamas**.

There were six hundred **cattle** on his ranch.
Many **people** were waiting outside.

The English **people** queue up at the bus-stop.
The **peoples** of Africa must be innumerable.

The **audience** applauded.
The **crowd** was very excited.
The **family** dates back to the 16th century.

goods	Waren
remains	Überreste
oats	Hafer
contents	Inhalt
thanks	Dank
riches	Reichtum
wages	Lohn
the Middle Ages	Mittelalter
surroundings	Umgebung

● Gegenstände (Dinge), die aus zwei gleichen Teilen bestehen

trousers	spectacles
shorts	glasses
jeans	goggles
pyjamas	binoculars
tights	scales
braces	scissors
pants	pincers

Beachte!

Soll die **Einzahl** dieser Substantive besonders betont werden, geht <u>some</u> oder <u>a pair of</u> voran.

● Immer im Plural stehen **cattle** und **people**

Beachte!

people .... die Leute
peoples .... das Volk, die Völker

Bei **Sammelbegriffen** steht das **Verb**

– in der **Einzahl**, wenn man an die Gruppe als Ganzes denkt

The Brown **family** go shopping every Friday afternoon.

The **government** are all on holiday.

The **crew** of the DC-9 are all experienced.

A **certain amount of** ⃞diligence⃞ is necessary.

A **great deal of** ⃞time⃞ was lost.

A **great number of** ⃞guests⃞ are expected.

Only **a few of** his ⃞books⃞ are really worth reading.

Plenty of time was wasted.
    ↑   ↑
      Singular

Plenty of postcards **were** written.
          ↑   ↑
            Plural

The children washed their **faces**. (Im D: ... das Gesicht)

Tom and Ann put on their **anoraks**. (Im D: ... ihren Anorak)

During the war many soldiers lost their **lives**. (Im D: ... das Leben)

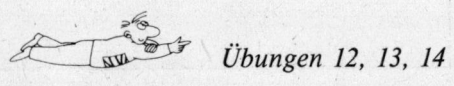

Übungen 12, 13, 14

- in der **Mehrzahl,** wenn man an die einzelnen Gruppenmitglieder denkt

army	crew	family	audience
class	team	company	parliament
crowd	group	police	government

Bei Mengenbezeichnungen mit „OF" steht das Verb

- in der **Einzahl** bei: a good deal of, a great deal of, a certain amount of, a bit of, ...

Anmerkung: es folgt jeweils ein Substantiv im Singular

- in der **Mehrzahl** bei: a number of, a few (of), a good many (of), ...

Anmerkung: es folgt jeweils ein Substantiv im Plural

- in der **Einzahl** oder **Mehrzahl** bei: plenty of, a lot of, lots of, part of ...

Anmerkung: die Zeitwortform hängt jeweils vom Numerus des Substantivs ab.

Im Plural stehen - abweichend vom Deutschen - die Bezeichnungen für

- Körperteile

- Kleidungsstücke

- life, death, health, mind ..., wenn sie sich auf mehrere Personen beziehen

"COMMON CASE" AND "POSSESSIVE CASE"

The girl prepares the steaks.
Subject (Common Case)

My **sister's** book is interesting.
Possessive Case

Dad gives his **sons** some pocket money.
      Indirect Object
    (Common Case)

The milkman delivers **the milk**.
      Direct Object
    (Common Case)

Tom's car, father's business, mother's friends ...

my brothers' bikes, my friends' toys ...
the children's homework, the women's rights ...

St. James' Park, Dickens' novels ...

my sister-in-law's flat, my mother-in-law's interests ...
That is someone else's business.

My sister's bike is in the garage.
My sisters' bikes are in the garage.
Everybody's friend is nobody's friend.
The birds' songs are most beautiful in spring.

2. „COMMON CASE" UND „POSSESSIVE CASE"

Die Fälle (Kasus) des Hauptworts:

Das Englische kennt nur zwei **Kasusformen,** den **Common Case** und den **Possessive Case.**
Das Substantiv erscheint als Subjekt und Objekt immer in der gleichen Form, im Common Case.
Die Beziehung zu den anderen Satzteilen wird durch die Wortstellung und / oder durch **Präpositionen** deutlich.
Um den Besitzer / Urheber einer Sache auszudrücken, wird der Possessive Case verwendet.

Bildung des Possessive Case:

- bei Substantiven
  im Singular ⟶ **Apostroph + s**

- bei Substantiven im Plural

  - nach Plural-s ⟶ **nur der Apostroph**
  - nach anderen Pluralendungen ⟶ **Apostroph + s**
  - nach Eigennamen auf „s" ⟶ **nur der Apostroph**
  - zusammengesetzte Substantive und zusammengehörige Wortgruppen werden als ein Wort behandelt

Gebrauch:

Der Possessive Case bezeichnet den Besitzer einer Sache oder den Urheber einer Handlung

- bei Personen und Tieren

You should study **Britain's** history more carefully.
Vienna's most remarkable cathedral is St. Stephan's.

Today's programme is said to be very amusing.
The plane covered the **380 miles'** distance in an hour.
He bought **a pound's** worth of petrol.

Tom **was at his wits' end** when the professor asked him a simple question.
For goodness' sake! What have you done?

This ⎡bike⎤ is mine and that is my **brother's**.

They bought all the new school things **at the stationer's**.
Every Sunday the children go to **St. Paul's**.
Tom stayed at **his uncle's** for two weeks.

Peter is a ⎡friend⎤ of **Tom's**.

Two ⎡friends⎤ of **Jane's** travelled to Sicily.

This ⎡play⎤ of **Priestley's** was filmed several times.

The legs **of** the table were painted.

A good harvest was the only hope **of** the poor.

In the days **of Richard the Lionhearted** many people joined the Crusades.
This is the car **of my friend,** who bought it last week.

- bei Personifizierungen (Staaten, Städte ...)

- bei Angaben der Zeit, des Maßes, des Werts ...

- in feststehenden Redewendungen wie

to be at one's wits' end	mit seiner Weisheit am Ende sein
to one's heart's content	nach Herzenslust
for goodness' sake	um Gottes willen
for pity's sake	um Himmels willen

Der Possessive Case steht **ohne** folgendes Bezugswort,

- wenn es aus dem Sinnzusammenhang erschlossen werden kann

- wenn damit **Geschäfte, Kaufhäuser, Kirchen, öffentliche Gebäude** oder **der Wohnsitz von Verwandten** gemeint sind (oft in Verbindung mit: at, to, from ...)

- wenn vor dem Bezugswort ein unbestimmter Artikel, ein Zahlwort, ein hinweisendes Fürwort steht, treten „OF + Possessive Case" hinter das Bezugswort.

Anstelle des Possessive Case steht die Wendung mit „OF"

- bei Substantiven, die k e i n e Lebewesen bezeichnen

- bei Sammelbegriffen und substantivierten Adjektiven

- bei Bezeichnungen für Einzelwesen, wenn es die Klarheit des Satzes erforderlich macht

the Archbishop **of** Canterbury, the Duke **of** Wellington, ...

the Battle **of** Trafalgar, the Treaty **of** Versailles,
the Congress **of** Vienna, ...

the Isle **of Man**, the State **of Washington**,
the month **of December**, ...

a cup of tea, a glass of water, a bottle of whisky, ...
each of you, all of us

He never left the village for **fear of** accident.
Everyone knows my **horror of** spiders.
His **love of** money makes him work day and night.
He was acquitted for **lack of** evidence.

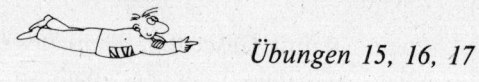

Übungen 15, 16, 17

- nach Titeln
- zur Angabe des Ortes geschichtlicher Ereignisse

- zur Verbindung von <u>Gattungsnamen</u> und **Eigennamen**
  nach: town, city, isle, state, month; rank, title, ...
- nach Substantiven und Pronomina, die eine Menge bezeichnen (vgl. nemo nostrum ... lat. Genitivus partitivus)
- in Wortverbindungen wie

fear of	Furcht vor
horror of	Abscheu vor
loss of	Verlust an
love of	Liebe zu
thought of	Gedanke an
lack of	Mangel an

ÜBUNGEN

8. *Es soll jeweils die fehlende männliche bzw. weibliche Form ergänzt werden!*

a) man – ...
b) ... – mistress
c) host – ...
d) ... – duchess
e) hero – ...
f) ... – sister
g) king – ...
h) ... – bitch
i) son – ...
j) ... – mother
k) bull (ox) – ...
l) ... – duck
m) gander – ...
n) ... – girl-friend
o) cock-robin – ...
p) ... – lioness

9. *Die fehlenden Fürwörter sollen ergänzt werden!*

a) They saw the Matterhorn and ... peak.

b) The English-teacher told the children about Scotland and ... people.

c) John's car is rather old, but ... is still too young to be called an "oldtimer".

d) The "Mayflower" was a sailboat. ... brought the Pilgrim Fathers to America.

e) Look, the moon! ... is high up in the sky.

f) Look at this jet. ... 's landing on the new runway.

g) Blacky is barking. Why is ... barking again?

h) Pussy is our lovely little cat. ... fur is soft.

i) Look! The cock-robin is flying to ... nest.

j) On this very day the sun was shining in all ... glory.

10. *Die folgenden Sätze sollen in die Mehrzahl gesetzt werden!*

a) There is one box on the shelf.

b) One loaf of bread and one tomato are left.

c) Tom's hobby is rather expensive.

d) One gentleman and one lady were waiting at the bus stop.

e) Tom disguised himself as a wolf. The children ...

f) Put this knife on the table.

g) The farmer has one goose, one calf, and one ox.

h) Joe took a very interesting photo.

11. Der vollständige Satz soll auf Englisch wiedergegeben werden!

a) All his _____ came to the party.
   (Freundinnen)

b) This play was written for the _____.
   (Zehnjährigen)

c) Leave all those _____ at home!
   (Stubenhocker)

d) She invited all her _____ to her birthday party.
   (Schwägerinnen)

e) The _____ applauded at the final curtain.
   (Zuschauer)

f) Take two _____ of milk.
   (Löffel voll)

12. Folgende Sätze sollen sinngemäß übersetzt werden!

a) Vielen Dank für dein Geschenk.

b) Die Dockarbeiter streiken für einen höheren Lohn.

c) Viele Burgen wurden während des Mittelalters errichtet.

d) Der Inhalt dieses Buches ist bemerkenswert.

e) Die Umgebung von Wien ist sehenswert.

f) Wo hast du diese Strumpfhose gekauft?

g) Gib mir diesen Feldstecher, bitte!

h) Gestern kaufte ich einen neuen Pyjama.

13. „Einzahl" oder „Mehrzahl"? Das Verb soll ergänzt werden!

a) The audience _____ applauding.
   (to be)

b) Our family _____ back to the 17th century.
   (to date)

c) When we arrived, the family _____ sitting round the fire.
   (to be)

d) The police _____ green uniforms.
   (to wear)

e) The crew of the "Atlantis" _____ very polite.
   (to be)

f) A great number of spectators _____ expected.
   (to be)

g) Plenty of time _____ wasted.
   (to be)

h) A certain amount of diligence _____ necessary.
   (to be)

14. Folgende Sätze sollen auf Englisch wiedergegeben werden!

a) Vor dem Schlafengehen waschen sich die Kinder die Hände und das Gesicht.

b) Die Kinder zogen den Anorak an und setzten die Mütze auf.

c) Acht Personen verloren bei diesem schrecklichen Unfall das Leben.

d) Sie waren total verrückt und verloren ihren Verstand.

15. Folgende Wörter sollen durch den „Possessive Case" verbunden werden!

a) Tom / car

b) my sisters / friends

c) glass / wine

d) bottle / beer

e) City / Vienna

f) today / programme

g) someone else / business

h) today / newspaper

16. *Der unterstrichene Satzteil soll jeweils im „Possessive Case" wiedergegeben werden!*

a) This is my house and that is <u>occupied by my parents</u>.

b) <u>The Church of St. Stephan</u> is the most interesting church in Vienna.

c) Whose car is this? I think it's <u>the one that belongs to Fred</u>.

d) Tom likes Verdi's operas but he does not like <u>those composed by Wagner</u>.

e) She has been staying at <u>the house of her friend</u> for a few days.

f) I have corrected Tom's homework, but where did you put <u>the one Pat wrote</u>?

17. *Folgende Sätze sollen sinngemäß wiedergegeben werden!*

a) In diesem Haus konnte sie nach Herzenslust singen und tanzen.

b) Fred war mit seiner Weisheit am Ende, als das Auto plötzlich stehen blieb.

c) Um Himmels willen! Was ist hier los?

d) Die Zwillinge haben ihren Geburtstag im Monat Dezember.

e) Joe wurde in Amerika geboren, im Staat Michigan.

THE PRONOUNS

PERSONAL PRONOUNS

I gave **you** the newspaper.
> I gave the newspaper **to you**.

You gave **him** the newspaper.
> You gave the newspaper **to him**.

He gave **her** the newspaper.
> He gave the newspaper **to her**.

She gave **us** the newspaper.
> She gave the newspaper **to us**.

We gave **you** the newspaper. (euch)
> We gave the newspaper **to you**.

You gave **them** the newspaper.
> You gave the newspaper **to them**.

They gave **me** the newspaper.
> They gave the newspaper **to me**.

Übung 18

DIE FÜRWÖRTER (PRONOMINA)

1. DIE PERSÖNLICHEN FÜRWÖRTER (PERSONALPRONOMINA)

		1. Fall	2. Fall	3. Fall	4. Fall
Einzahl	ICH 1. Person	I ich	of me meiner	(to) me mir	me mich
	DU 2. Person	you du	of you deiner	(to) you dir	you dich
	ER 3. Person	he er	of him seiner	(to) him ihm	him ihn
	SIE 3. Person	she sie	of her ihrer	(to) her ihr	her sie
	ES 3. Person	it es	of it seiner	(to) it ihm	it es
Mehrzahl	WIR 1. Person	we wir	of us unser	(to) us uns	us uns
	IHR 2. Person	you ihr	of you euer	(to) you euch	you euch
	SIE 3. Person	they sie	of them ihrer	(to) them ihnen	them sie

Beachte die beiden Formen des 3. Falls in nebenstehenden Sätzen!

Im ersten Satz liegt die Bedeutung jeweils auf „Zeitung", im zweiten Satz auf „dir", „ihm", „ihr" ...

Who's that <u>girl</u>? **She's** a friend of mine. (Im D: **Es** ist ... **Das** ist ...)
Who are <u>the boys</u> in this picture? **They** are my classmates.

Who's at the door? **It's** the milkman.
Is **it** Ann and Nelly? No, **it's** the boys.

Is **it** <u>raining</u>? No, **it's** <u>snowing</u>.
It's <u>ten o'clock</u> and we've still got a lot of work to do.
<u>How far</u> is **it** to Eastham? **It's** just <u>a ten minutes' walk</u>.

I'm glad to meet you.
How are you? **I'm fine**, thanks.
I'm sorry for not having written sooner.
He succeeded in writing novels.

<u>She's studying hard</u> though **it** may be rather difficult for her.
<u>The children are here again</u> and I'm very happy of **it**.

It is <u>he</u> who won the race.
It is <u>they</u> who solved the mistery.
It is <u>we</u> who are playing records.

There are fourteen girls in our class.
There is only one apple-tree in our garden.

Will it be cold tomorrow? **I'm afraid so.** (Ich befürchte es.)
Will it be fine tomorrow? **I hope so.**
Does she know you are in Vienna? I don't **think so.**

„ES" im Englischen wird wiedergegeben

- durch „he / she / they" → Hinweis auf <u>vorher genannte Personen</u>

Beachte!

Bei noch nicht genannten oder unbekannten Personen steht „it" (auch in der Mehrzahl)!

- durch „it"

  • bei der Angabe von <u>Witterung, Zeit, Entfernung</u>

Beachte!

„ES" im Deutschen → persönliche Ausdrucksweise im Englischen

es freut mich .... I'm glad
es geht mir gut .... I'm fine
es tut mir leid .... I'm sorry
es gelingt mir .... I succeed in

  • als Hinweis auf eine <u>vorhergehende Wortgruppe</u> oder einen <u>vorhergehenden Satz</u>

  • zur Hervorhebung <u>einzelner Satzglieder</u>

- durch „there is / there are" im Sinne von „Es gibt..." hinweisend auf das nachfolgende Subjekt

- durch „so" hinweisend auf einen vorhergehenden Satz nach Verben wie

  „to be afraid, to believe, to expect, to hope, to say, to suppose, to think ..."

Who can **guess**? (... kann es erraten?)
How do you **know**? (... weißt du es?)
Mum **told** me. (... erzählte es mir.)
I think it's rather difficult, but I'll **try**. (... es versuchen.)

One should love **one's** neighbour as **oneself**.

In England **people** celebrate Christmas on the twenty-fifth of December.
People say that Molly is a clever girl.

She didn't mind what **they** called her.

The doctor was sent for. (**Man** schickte ...)
Discos are found everywhere. (**Man** findet ...)

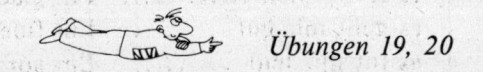

Übungen 19, 20

- kein Pronomen steht – abweichend vom Deutschen – nach Wörtern wie

   „to guess, to explain, to know, to tell, to try, ..."

„MAN" (allgemeines Pronomen) wird im Englischen wiedergegeben

- durch das unbestimmte Fürwort **„one"** (in allgemeingültigen Aussagen und Sprichwörtern)
- durch **„people"**
- durch **„we / you / they"**
- durch das **„persönliche Passiv"** (vgl. Bd. 1, S. 131)

POSSESSIVE PRONOUNS

Is this **my** book? – No, it's **mine**.

Is this **your** pen? – No, it's **yours**.

Is this **his** hat? – Yes, it's **his**.

Is this **her** ball? – Yes, it's **hers**.

Is this **its** nest? – Yes, it's **its**. (own)

Is this **our** car? – Yes, it's **ours**.

Is this **your** bike? – Yes, it's **yours**.

Is this **their** house? – Yes, it's **theirs**.

Übung 21

Blow **your** nose!
Jim broke **his** arm.
I put on **my** trousers and **my** warm pullover.

The children took **their** bikes and off they went.
Fifty miners lost **their** lives.

2. DIE BESITZANZEIGENDEN FÜRWÖRTER (POSSESSIVPRONOMINA)

Einzahl	1. Person	MEIN	my book	mine
Einzahl	2. Person	DEIN	your pen	yours
Einzahl	3. Person	SEIN	his hat	his
Einzahl	3. Person	IHR	her ball	hers
Einzahl	3. Person	SEIN	its nest	its (own)
Mehrzahl	1. Person	UNSER	our car	ours
Mehrzahl	2. Person	EUER	your bike	yours
Mehrzahl	3. Person	IHR	their house	theirs

↑ immer **vor** einem Hauptwort

↑ auf ein vorhergehendes Hauptwort bezogen

Verallgemeinernd: one's / one's own

Gebrauch des adjektivischen Possessivpronomens:

Zum Ausdruck der Zugehörigkeit

– bei Körperteilen, Kleidungsstücken

– bei „house, bicycle, car, work ... life, death, mind ..."

The teacher took the boy by the arm.
                   ↓
                Object

The boy was taken by the arm.
 ↓
Subject

Do you like this house? It's **my own**.
The poet is reading **his own** poems.

I have a house **of my own**.
He has not many books **of his own**.
Mr Greenwood is a rich man. He has five houses **of his own**.

Your opinions and **my** opinions are just the same.
Your opinions and **mine** are just the same.

I can give you a book **of mine**.
Tom was at the cinema with some (with three) friends **of his**.
This house **of theirs** is rather old.

Yours sincerely, **Yours** truly, **Yours** faithfully, ...

The little robin flew to another bird's nest, not to **its own**.

Übungen 22, 23

Beachte den bestimmten Artikel, wenn die besitzende Person

- <u>Objekt</u> ist

- <u>Subjekt</u> eines passiven Satzes ist

Das adjektivische Possessivpronomen wird **verstärkt** durch

- ein nachgestelltes „**own**" (Im D: „eigen", „selbst", ...)
- „**of ... own**" (nachgestellt), wenn vor dem Substantiv ein <u>unbestimmter Artikel</u>, ein <u>unbestimmtes Fürwort</u> oder ein <u>Zahlwort</u> steht.

Gebrauch des substantivischen Possessivpronomens:

- **aus stilistischen Gründen,** um die Verbindung zweier adjektivischer Possessivpronomina mit <u>„and"</u> zu vermeiden
- **of + substantivisches Possessivpronomen** (nachgestellt), wenn vor dem Substantiv ein <u>unbestimmter Artikel</u>, ein <u>unbestimmtes Fürwort</u>, ein <u>Zahlwort</u> oder ein <u>hinweisendes Fürwort</u> steht.
- „**yours**" in Briefen als Höflichkeitsformel

Beachte!
„Its" erscheint vielfach in der Wendung „its own".

REFLEXIVE PRONOUNS

Reflexive Use:

I disguise **myself** as Robin Hood.

Look at **yourself**.

She was not thinking of **herself**.

He saw **himself** in the mirror.

It (the dog) dried **itself**.

We helped **ourselves** to some sausage.

You disguise **yourselves** as Charles and Diana.

They helped **themselves** to some more biscuits.

Emphatic Use:

I sewed the skirt **myself**.

You **yourself** told me that.

The President **himself** came to the exhibition.

Granny lives by **herself**.

The little bird made the nest all by **itself**.

We repaired the car **ourselves**.

You translated these sentences all by **yourselves**.

They tried the medicine **themselves**.

One should love one's neighbour as **oneself**.

Übung 24

I dressed **myself** <u>carefully</u> for Sue's birthday party.

I washed and dressed <u>quickly</u>.

3. DIE RÜCKBEZÜGLICHEN FÜRWÖRTER (REFLEXIVPRONOMINA)

Im Gegensatz zum Deutschen verwendet das Englische <u>nicht so häufig</u> das Reflexivpronomen.

Zum Vergleich:

This book reads well .... liest **sich** gut.
It happened years ago ...... es ereignete **sich** ...
Attention! A fox is approaching .... nähert **sich**.

Singular	1. Person	MICH	myself	
	2. Person	DICH	yourself	
	3. Person	SICH	himself	„SELBST", „SELBER", „(GANZ) ALLEIN"
	3. Person	SICH	herself	
	3. Person	SICH	itself	
Plural	1. Person	UNS	ourselves	
	2. Person	EUCH	yourselves	
	3. Person	SICH	themselves	

↑ reflexive Bedeutung   ↑ emphatische Bedeutung

Verallgemeinernd: **onself**

Gebrauch als Reflexivpronomen:

– abweichend vom Deutschen werden einige Verben mit oder ohne Reflexivpronomen gebraucht: wash, dress, shave
  - ● **mit** Reflexivpronomen → der <u>bewußte Vorgang</u> der Handlung wird ausgedrückt
  - ● **ohne** Reflexivpronomen → der <u>gewohnheitsmäßige Ablauf</u> wird ausgedrückt

The children are playing hide-and-seek. Tom **is hiding himself** in the cupboard.
The student **proved himself** very intelligent.
The first immigrants **settled** along the coast.

Many people don't **care for** politics.
Mr Smith **decided** to leave London.
He's a good fellow. You can **rely on** him.
You can't **imagine** how interesting Windsor Castle is.
The children **are looking forward to** the holidays.
Do you **remember** her last birthday party?
Robin Hood and his men had to **withdraw** when they saw the Sheriff of Nottingham.

Mrs Brown **was** mistaken. (... irrte **sich**)
Mary **got** engaged to Bob. (... verlobte **sich**)
It was bright and sunny but suddenly it **became** cloudy. (... es bewölkte **sich**)
Last winter she had an accident and her leg **grew** stiff. (... versteifte **sich**)

Verben, die **mit** oder **ohne** Reflexivpronomen gebraucht werden:

to assemble (oneself)	sich versammeln
to feel (oneself)	sich fühlen
to hide (oneself)	sich verstecken
to prepare (oneself)	sich vorbereiten
to prove (oneself)	sich erweisen
to settle (oneself)	sich ansiedeln
to spread (oneself)	sich ausbreiten
to submit (oneself)	sich unterwerfen
to surrender (oneself)	sich ergeben
to trouble (oneself)	sich beunruhigen

– abweichend vom Deutschen verwendet das Englische nichtreflexive Verben wie

to amount to	sich belaufen auf
to approach	sich nähern
to care for	sich kümmern um
to change	sich ändern
to complain of	sich beklagen über
to decide	sich entschließen
to rely on	sich verlassen auf
to differ	sich unterscheiden
to fancy	sich einbilden
to imagine	sich vorstellen
to happen	sich ereignen
to join	sich anschließen
to lie down	sich hinlegen
to long for	sich sehnen nach
to look forward to	sich freuen auf
to meet	sich treffen
to move	sich bewegen
to refuse	sich weigern
to remember	sich erinnern
to sit down	sich (hin)setzen
to withdraw	sich zurückziehen
to wonder at	sich wundern über

– zur Vermeidung des Reflexivpronomens stehen folgende Konstruktionen

to be	
to get	+ Past Participle /
to become	Adjective /
to grow	Adverb

Just imagine that! I met Mr Brown **himself**.
I **myself** will be there.

I'll be there **myself**.

Can you translate this letter **by yourself**?
Little Betty sewed this dress **by herself**.

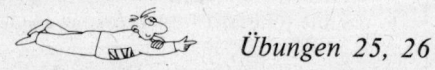

Übungen 25, 26

RECIPROCAL PRONOUNS

They should help **one another**.
At the party the guests got to know **one another**.

Ann and Pat were angry for a long time, but finally they greeted **each other**.

Übung 27

DEMONSTRATIVE PRONOUNS

This (here) is my brother Joe. **That** (over there) is my brother Jim.

These are my new shoes. **Those** are my old shoes.

Gebrauch als emphatisches Pronomen:

- zur Hervorhebung von Personen und Dingen → unmittelbar hinter dem Wort, das hervorgehoben werden soll
- zur Hervorhebung des Subjekts → auch am Satzende
- in der Bedeutung „(ganz) allein, ohne Hilfe" **(all) by oneself**

4. DIE PRONOMINA DER GEGENSEITIGKEIT (REZIPROKE PRONOMINA)

Ein gegenseitiges Verhältnis wird ausgedrückt durch

one another	SICH (EINANDER) allgemeingültige, sachliche Aussage
each other	SICH (GEGENSEITIG, EINER DEN ANDEREN) persönlich; vor allem, wenn es sich um zwei Personen handelt

5. DIE HINWEISENDEN FÜRWÖRTER (DEMONSTRATIVPRONOMINA)

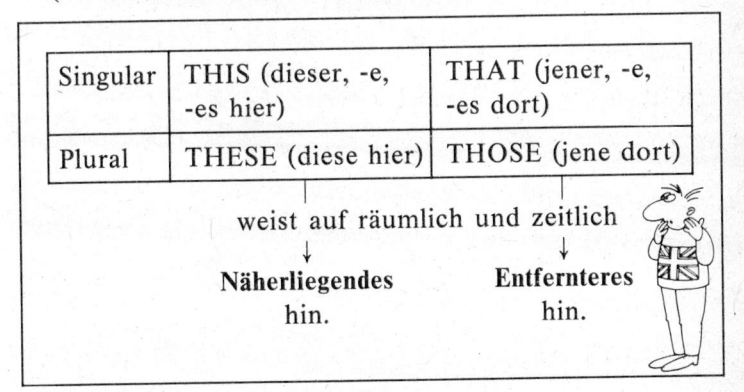

Singular	THIS (dieser, -e, -es hier)	THAT (jener, -e, -es dort)
Plural	THESE (diese hier)	THOSE (jene dort)

weist auf räumlich und zeitlich

↓ **Näherliegendes** hin.

↓ **Entfernteres** hin.

This girl is Mary. **That** girl is Jane.
These books here are new. **Those** over there are old.

This skirt is just the right size. I'll take it.
I don't like **that** colour, it's unfashionable.

This boy is tall, **that** <u>one</u> is even taller.

This girl is intelligent, that **one** is more intelligent.

This pen is Nelly's, that (**one**) is Jane's.

These books are interesting, those are boring.

Listen to **this**!
Did you know about **that**?

Gebrauch:

– adjektivisch, als Hinweis auf Personen oder Dinge

Achtung!

THIS, THESE: bezeichnen auch Zustimmung

THAT, THOSE: bezeichnen auch Ablehnung

Beachte das Demonstrativpronomen in der Gegenüberstellung!

Aus stilistischen Gründen wird das Substantiv durch das **unbestimmte Fürwort „ONE"** ersetzt.

Das „Stützwort" (PROP-WORD)
- **muß** bei Personen in der Einzahl verwendet werden
- **kann** bei Dingen in der Einzahl verwendet werden
- wird **nicht verwendet** in der Mehrzahl

– substantivisch in der Bedeutung „dies – das", „dieses – jenes"

Beachte die Redewendungen!

this morning / evening	**heute** morgen / abend
this week / month / year	**in** dieser Woche, **in** diesem Monat, **in** diesem Jahr
in these days	heutzutage
in those days	damals
That's it!	Richtig! Gut!
That'll do!	Genug! Das reicht!
That's all right!	Das ist recht!
that's why ...	deshalb
that's how he got it	**so** hat er es bekommen

Such is life.

Such a handsome young man! = he is a <u>very</u> handsome young man.

The children had **such** (much) fun during their stay in Brighton.

All sorts of vegetables were sold **such as** carrots, beans, cauliflower, cabbage ...

That (the) girl **who** won the race will get a prize.
Those (the) persons **who** speak two languages will have a chance to get the job.

That (the) district of Vienna **which** is called "The City" is most interesting
Those (the) cars **which** I tested were too expensive.

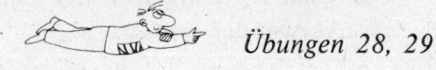

Übungen 28, 29

INTERROGATIVE PRONOUNS

Who wrote this poem?
Whose book is this?
Who(m) did you meet?
With whom did you meet her?

What is in this box?
What papers do you read?
To what is this notice referring?

Which of these novels do you like best?
Which do you like better, wine or beer?
Which of Vienna's theatres are most popular?

Beachte den Gebrauch von „SUCH"!

- mit hinweisendem Charakter „so, von dieser Art"
- „such a ..." zur Bezeichnung eines <u>hohen Grades</u>

- im Sinne von „much"

- „such as" vor Aufzählungen

Beachte die **determinative (näher bestimmende) Funktion** in folgenden Wendungen
- „that (those) ... who" in bezug auf Personen

- „that (those) ... which" in bezug auf Dinge

6. DIE FRAGEFÜRWÖRTER (INTERROGATIVPRONOMINA)

Substantivischer Gebrauch:

	Frage nach		
	Personen	Dingen	Personen und Dingen
1. Fall	who?	what?	which?
2. Fall	whose?	–	–
3. und 4. Fall mit Präpositionen	whom? (who?) of whom? to whom? with whom?	what? of what? to what? with what?	which? of which? to which? with which?

75

Whom do you know in Brighton?
Who do you know?

What girl could be so silly?
In what year did the Coopers move to Reading?

Which of these girls is prettiest?
Which of the books is most interesting?

For whom are you <u>waiting</u>?
   Who are you <u>waiting</u> **for**?
With what are you <u>writing</u>?
   What are you <u>writing</u> **with**?
At what are you <u>laughing</u>?
   What are you <u>laughing</u> **at**?

Übung 30

What colour is your new coat?
What colour are Tom's trousers?

What are these tools used **for**?
What age are the Cooper twins?
What is "Interrogative Pronoun" **in** German?

When did the children leave?

Where are all my books? (Wo?)
Where are you going **to**? (Wohin?)
Where did the Kennedys come **from**? (Woher)

Why are you late today?

How did you get there?
How long did you stay there?
How many folk songs do you know?
How much is this blouse?

Übungen 31, 32

Beachte!

- „Spoken English" verwendet anstelle von „whom" vielfach „who"

- den **adjektivischen Gebrauch** von „what" und „which"

  WHAT fragt im allgemeinen Sinn nach Personen und Dingen

  WHICH (OF) trifft eine Auswahl aus einer bestimmten Anzahl von Personen und Dingen

- die Stellung der **Präposition** im Fragesatz: „Everyday English" setzt die **Präposition** nach dem Verb

Achte auf folgende Redewendungen!

What's the time, please?	
What colour is / are ...?	Welche Farbe **hat / haben** ...?
What ... for?	Wozu ...?
What age ...?	Wie alt ...?
What is ... in German / French ...?	Was heißt ... auf deutsch / französisch ...

Weitere Interrogativpronomina:

WHEN fragt nach einer Zeitergänzung

WHERE fragt nach einer Ortsergänzung

WHY fragt nach dem Grund

HOW fragt nach der Art und Weise; oft in Verbindung mit „How long ...? How many ...? How much ...?"

RELATIVE PRONOUNS

Here is the man **who** kept house.
Here is the girl **whose** sister goes to school in Vienna.
Here is the boy **whom** I wanted to help.
The man **to whom** she gave the book was about forty years old.

The film **which** is on today is an Italian one.
Here is the dog **whose** master died. (... the master **of which** ...)
This is the dog **to which** we gave some bones.

Pussy, **who** quickly caught a mouse, is a very clever little cat.
Cambridge, **to whom** she owed so much, honoured her for her studying.

She looks like a teacher, **which** in fact she is.
The student was asked many questions, **which** he didn't like at all.

Here are Mr Brown and his new car **that** we saw in town yesterday.

The girl, **that** (who) we met yesterday, was my cousin.
The book **that** you lent me was very interesting.

This is the tallest building **that** I've ever seen.
This is the best poem **that** I've ever read.
All **that** she said was untrue.
Aunt Emily bought everything **that** was expensive.
There isn't much left **that** we could offer you.

7. DIE BEZÜGLICHEN FÜRWÖRTER (RELATIVPRONOMINA)

	Bezogen auf		
	Personen	Dinge	Personen und Dinge
1. Fall	who	which	that
2. Fall	whose	whose (of which)	–
Objektform mit Präposition	whom? of whom to whom	which of which to which	that (that … of) (that … to)

Beachte den Gebrauch von

– WHO …… bezogen auf Personen, Haustiere und personifizierte Länder

– WHICH … bezogen auf Dinge oder Begriffe und auf den Inhalt eines vorhergehenden Satzes

– THAT ….. bezogen auf Personen und Dinge (gemeinsam)

Beachte!

„THAT" - **kann** anstelle von „who" und „which" verwendet werden; der Gebrauch von „who" für Personen ist allerdings üblicher

- **muß** verwendet werden
  ● nach Superlativen

  ● nach „all, everything, any(thing), some(thing), nothing, much, little, …"

Tom is a clever boy, and, **what** is more important, he is also very diligent.

What made her sad was that he left her.

This was the best film **that** I have ever seen.
↓
Personal Pronoun

This was the best film I've ever seen.

This is the boy **who** won the prize.
↓
Verb

This is the most interesting topic that I've ever heard **about**.

Here is the man (whom) I was talking to.

Where is the girl you were talking to?

Jim, who reads a lot of books , knows quite a lot about modern literature.

This book reminds me of the time **when** I was a little girl.

This is the house **where** I spent my childhood.

I think you can understand the reason **why** I don't like to meet her.

Übungen 33, 34, 35, 36, 37, 38, 39, 40

„**WHAT**" kann anstelle eines Relativpronomens stehen
- bezogen auf einen nachfolgenden Satz (D: was)

- in einer näher bestimmten Funktion im Sinne von „that which ..." (D: das, was ...)

Beachte!

Das **Relativpronomen**
- kann weggelassen werden, wenn ihm ein Hauptwort oder ein persönliches Fürwort folgt

- darf NICHT weggelassen werden, wenn ihm ein Verb folgt.

Achte auf

- die Stellung der **Präposition** nach der Verbgruppe , wenn der Relativsatz mit „that" oder ohne Relativpronomen angeschlossen ist

- die Beistrichsetzung im bestimmenden bzw. erläuternden Relativsatz (s. Bd. 1, S. 35)

Beachte die relativen Anknüpfungen mit
- **WHEN** ... nach Zeitangaben

- **WHERE** ... nach Ortsangaben
- **WHY** ... nach Angaben des Grundes

INDEFINITE PRONOUNS

There is **some** <u>wine</u> in the bottle.
               ↓
       Singular

Have you got **any** <u>apples</u>?
               ↓
       Plural

I'd like **some** chocolate. I haven't **any** chocolate.

We bought **some** fine presents for the children.

There are **some** plates on the table.
I'd like some coffee.

He never comes without bringing **some** flowers.

Have you got **some** carrots? <u>Yes, of course.</u>

Joe hasn't **any** friends.
Have you got **any** interesting stamps?

If I had **any** stamps, I'd show them to you.

8. DIE UNBESTIMMTEN FÜRWÖRTER (INDEFINITPRONOMINA)

SOME – ANY

... bezeichnen eine bestimmte Anzahl oder Menge von Personen oder Dingen.

Bedeutung:

In Verbindung

– mit der Einzahl („etwas")

– mit der Mehrzahl („einige", „irgendwelche")

„SOME – ANY" (adjektivisch) bezeichnen

– eine unbestimmte Menge im Singular
– eine unbestimmte Anzahl im Plural.

„SOME" steht

– in positiven Sätzen und Aufforderungen

– in verneinten Sätzen mit positivem Sinn
– in Fragesätzen, wenn eine positive Antwort erwartet wird.

„ANY" steht

– in verneinten Sätzen
– in Fragesätzen, wenn die Antwort ungewiß ist
– in Konditionalsätzen (If-Sätzen)

Some agreed, some disagreed.
Look at these beautiful flowers! Would you like some?
Give me some money, please. – If I had any, I'd give you some.

Is there anybody at the door?
There's somebody at the door.
Anything else?
Someone will have to do that difficult job.
Somehow we'll find our way through the bushes.
Sometimes I'd like to live in the country.

Übungen 41, 42

Every house must have a chimney.
Every Englishman carries an umbrella.
Every winter the Coopers go skiing in Austria.

Mike and Mary meet every other day.
Jim and Joe play tennis every four days.
Old Mrs Brown must take her medicine every three hours.
They go to a concert every now and then.

Everybody will help you.
Everyone in class is busy preparing the party.
Everything must be finished before 10 o'clock.

„SOME – ANY" (substantivisch) bezeichnen eine unbestimmte Anzahl

Die **zusammengesetzten Formen** werden wie „some" und „any" gebraucht:

somebody   – anybody (jemand)
someone   – anyone (irgend jemand)
something – anything (irgend etwas)
somewhere – anywhere (irgendwo)
somehow   – anyhow (irgendwie)
sometimes (manchmal)

EVERY – EACH (OF) – ANY

„**EVERY**" (nur adjektivisch)

– steht vor Substantiven im Singular als verallgemeinernde Aussage → auf eine unbestimmte Anzahl bezogen

Beachte die Redewendungen!

every other day	jeden zweiten Tag
every four days	jeden vierten Tag
every three hours	alle drei Stunden
every now and then	von Zeit zu Zeit, dann und wann

Zusammengesetzte Formen:

everybody ⎫
everyone ⎭ jeder
everything   alles
everywhere   überall

Each boy here must study Latin.
Each dress here must be shortened.
Each of these cars is a Ford.
The headmaster spoke to **each** of us.

These blouses are **5 £ each.**

These scarves are **10 $ each.**

You may choose **any** cake you like.
Tim can answer **any** question the teacher asks.
Any of the dictionaries will do.
You may use **any of** the glasses.

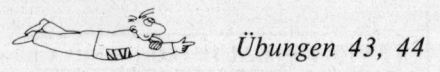

Übungen 43, 44

They stayed in the city **all** day long.

All the guests came at 4.

All that glitters isn't gold.

All of us went skiing last winter.

The guide showed us the **whole** country.
We travelled round the **whole** of Austria.

„EACH": adjektivisch und substantivisch (each of)
- auf eine bestimmte (begrenzte) Anzahl bezogen, genau umschriebene Gruppen von Personen, Dingen, ...

Beachte die Redewendungen:

5 £ each   je 5 Pfund

10 $ each   je 10 Dollar

„ANY (OF)": in der Bedeutung „jeder beliebige"

ALL - WHOLE

„ALL"
- adjektivisch; bezeichnet ein Ganzes

  Bedeutung:

  In Verbindung
  - mit der Einzahl („ganz")
  - mit der Mehrzahl („alle")

- substantivisch
  - im Singular („alles")
  - im Plural („alle")

„WHOLE": bezeichnet ein ungeteiltes Ganzes; betont die Ganzheit stärker als „all"

The children stayed at the seaside **all day long**.
All in all it was a success.
"I must tell you **once for all**: Write more carefully!"
They walked through the woods and **all of a sudden** a fox appeared from behind the bushes.
First of all I must tell you the latest news.

You can't go to the cinema this evening, that's **beyond all question**.

At the beginning the film was a bit boring, but **on the whole** it was rather amusing.

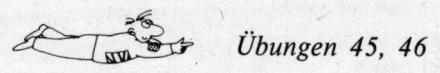

Übungen 45, 46

Both girls are very diligent.
They **both** accepted gratefully.

The two Cooper children are very different.
The two men are enemies.

Either of the boys spent his holidays in London.
Who will win the match? I don't know, **either** may win.

Vienna is situated <u>on</u> **either** side of the Danube.
There are trees <u>on</u> **either** side of the avenue.

Neither of the boys is right.

Übung 47

Beachte die Redewendungen!

all day long	den ganzen Tag
all the better	um so besser
all in all	im ganzen gesehen
after all	schließlich, trotzdem
not at all	durchaus nicht
once for all	ein für allemal
all of a sudden	ganz plötzlich
all but (one)	alle außer (einen)
first (last) of all	zuallererst (zuallerletzt)
all at once	auf einmal
beyond all question	ganz außer Frage
it's all the same	das ist mir ganz gleich
a whole lot of	eine ganze Menge
on the whole	im großen und ganzen

BOTH – THE TWO – EITHER – NEITHER

„BOTH": adjektivisch und substantivisch („beide"); betont die Zusammengehörigkeit zweier Personen oder Dinge

„THE TWO": „beide", die Zusammengehörigkeit bleibt unbetont bzw. Gegensätzlichkeit wird ausgedrückt

„EITHER": adjektivisch und substantivisch, „beide", „jeder von beiden", „der eine oder der andere" (von zweien)

Beachte!

Nach Präpositionen hat „either" die Bedeutung von „both"

„NEITHER": „beide nicht", „keiner von beiden", „weder der eine noch der andere"

The children climbed the mountain, **one** in front of the other.

Tom lives on the **other** side of the river.
I don't like this skirt; show me the **other** (one).
Jack and Joe went cycling, the **others** went boating.

Show me **another** <u>pullover</u>, please.
I'd like **another** <u>glass</u> of wine.

If this coat doesn't fit, try **another**.

Don't be so unfriendly. There must be a **different** way of telling her the truth.

Somebody else will show you the castle.
May I show you **something else**?
They filed in **one after the other**.
Somehow or other it will come to an end.

Übung 48

No pupil passed the test.
No smoking.

Is there any coffee? No, there is **none**.
None of his friends came to the party.

ONE - OTHER - ANOTHER

„ONE": adjektivisch und substantivisch
- in bezug auf zwei Personen oder Dinge wird der (die, das) erste mit „one" bezeichnet

„OTHER": adjektivisch und substantivisch

„ANOTHER"
- MIT Substantiv in der Bedeutung „noch ein", „ein zweiter", „ein weiterer", ...
- OHNE Substantiv in der Bedeutung „ein anderer", „ein neuer", ...

Achtung!
„DIFFERENT": anders, ein anderer, im Sinne von „andersartig"

Beachte die Redewendungen!

somebody else	jemand anderer
something else	etwas anderes
the other day	neulich
some time or other	doch einmal
one after the other	einer nach dem anderen
somehow or other	irgendwie

NO − NONE - NO ONE - NOBODY - NOTHING

„NO":   adjektivisch („kein")

„NONE": substantivisch („kein, -e, -es"), auf ein vorhergehendes oder folgendes Substantiv bezogen

No one failed to notice his talent.

Nobody helped him with his work.

Did you buy anything? – No, **nothing**.

We <u>don't tell</u> **anyone**.
She <u>didn't buy</u> **anything**.

Übung 49

„NO ONE"
„NOBODY" } „niemand", „keiner"

„NOTHING": „nichts"

Beachte den Gebrauch von „anyone", „anybody", „anything" im verneinten Satz!

The teacher did**n't** correct **many** exercises.

I haven't got **much** money.
That's really asked too **much.**

Little Tommy hasn't got **many** toys.
There weren't **many** guests at John's party.

Mr Smith has **a lot of** money.
Lots of children were playing in the park.

We've lost **a good deal of** time.
There's **a great deal** of bread at home.

Study these rules **several** times.
A large number of tourists crossed the border at Sillian.

She bought **few** apples. → She did**n't** buy **many** apples.

Mr Brown earns very **little** money.
I'll just take **a little** sugar.

There are too **few** flowers in our garden.
She bought **a few** apples.

Übung 50, 51

MUCH - MANY - LITTLE - FEW

... adjektivisch und substantivisch gebraucht.

Beachte die Steigerung!

much ⎫
many ⎭ – more – most

little – less – least
few – fewer – fewest

„MUCH - MANY": werden vorwiegend in verneinten Sätzen und Fragesätzen gebraucht.

„MUCH": bezeichnet eine große Menge; die einzelnen Elemente sind nicht zählbar → „viel"

„MANY": bezeichnet eine große Anzahl; die einzelnen Elemente sind zählbar ⟶ „viele"

Beachte die Ersatzformen in positiven Sätzen für

– „much" und „many" ⟶ a lot of, lots of, plenty of

– „much" ⟶ a good deal of, a great deal of

– „many" ⟶ several, a (large) number of

„LITTLE - FEW": werden vorwiegend in positiven Sätzen gebraucht. In negativen Sätzen steht vielfach ein verneintes Verb mit „much" oder „many".

„LITTLE": bezeichnet eine geringe Menge; die einzelnen Elemente sind nicht zählbar ⟶ „wenig"
   „a little": ein wenig, etwas

„FEW": bezeichnet eine geringe Anzahl; die einzelnen Elemente sind zählbar ⟶ „wenige"
   „a few": einige, ein paar

ÜBUNGEN

18. Folgende Sätze sollen auf Englisch wiedergegeben werden!

a) Unser armer Blacky! Wer wird sich seiner annehmen?

b) Sie ist ein intelligentes Mädchen – Und wie sich ihre Eltern ihrer rühmen!

c) Mach dich nicht lustig über sie! Sie sind arm.

d) Hast du ihm eine Ansichtskarte geschrieben?

e) Dieser Hut gehört nicht mir, er gehört ihr.

f) Sie gaben ihm das Geschenk, nicht mir.

g) Er schickte mir ein Paket zu meinem Geburtstag.

h) Er versprach ihnen einen Ausflug nach Salzburg.

i) Wir schickten ihnen Kleider, Lebensmittel und Spielsachen.

j) Wem gehören diese Fahrräder? Sie gehören uns.

k) Hat euch der Lehrer das Buch über Australien geliehen?

l) Biete ihr den Kuchen an! Er wird ihr schmecken.

19. Der vollständige Satz soll auf Englisch wiedergegeben werden!

a) _____ five apple-trees and ten plum-trees in our garden.
   (Es gibt)

b) _____ only one girl in that group.
   (Es gibt)

c) I couldn't come earlier, _____.
   (es tut mir leid)

d) It's going to rain. _____.
   (Ich befürchte es)

e) I'll come at four today. – _____.
   (Hoffentlich)

f) _____ to meet you after a long time.
   (Es freut mich)

g) How are you? _____, thanks.
   (Es geht mir gut)

h) _____ in convincing him.
   (Es gelang ihr)

i) I think I can't help you, but I'll _____.
   (es versuchen)

j) _____ that he is very diligent.
   (Man sagt)

k) _____ to knit all her pullovers herself.
   (Man sagt)

l) _____.
   (Man schickte nach der Rettung)

20. Das unterstrichene Wort soll besonders hervorgehoben werden!

a) <u>Er</u> brachte den Brief.

b) <u>Sie</u> gewannen den Wettbewerb.

c) <u>Wir</u> machten so einen Lärm.

d) <u>Sie</u> schrieb diesen Brief.

21. Der folgende Satz soll in alle Personen gesetzt werden!

This fountain-pen belongs to me, it's mine.

22. Folgende Sätze sollen auf Englisch sinngemäß wiedergegeben werden!

a) Putz dir die Nase und zieh den Pullover an!

b) Was für ein Unfall! Tom brach sich den Arm, Fred und Jack brachen sich das Bein.

c) Eine Schlagzeile: 20 Passagiere verloren das Leben.

d) Er stieg in das Auto und fuhr los.

e) Er setzte sich nieder und begann sofort mit der Arbeit.

f) Wasch dir die Hände vor dem Abendessen!

g) Dieses Mädchen hat ihm den Kopf verdreht.

h) Es ist sehr heiß hier; zieh dir den Mantel aus.

i) Gib die Hände aus der Tasche, wenn du mit mir sprichst.

j) Mir tut der Kopf weh.

k) Sie fuhr sich mit den Fingern durchs Haar und faßte einen Entschluß.

l) Gib mir die Pfote, Blacky!

23. Es sollen Sätze nach folgendem Muster gebildet werden!

> This is your idea. – This is the idea of yours.

a) Where did you hide my books?

b) His new teacher is very kind.

c) Would you mind showing me your photo?

d) I'd like to see the Smiths' new car.

e) Their house was rather expensive.

f) Joe went skating with his three friends.

24. Folgende Sätze sollen in alle Personen gesetzt werden!

a) I disguise myself as a clown.

b) I'll repair the car myself.

25. Folgende Sätze sollen sinngemäß wiedergegeben werden!

a) Sie näherten sich der Küste als das Benzin ausging.

b) Ich werde dir erzählen, was sich ereignet hat.

c) Lehrer und Kinder freuen sich auf die Ferien.

d) Beweg' dich nicht!

e) Sie beklagten sich über die niedrigen Löhne.

f) Ich bin sehr müde, ich möchte mich hinlegen.

g) Sie trafen sich zufällig an der Haltestelle.

h) Sie schlossen sich dieser Partei an.

26. Es soll jeweils „SELBST" ergänzt werden!

a) The President ... came to open the fair.

b) She'll be there ...

c) What a surprise! I met the Coopers ...

d) You ... told me that.

e) We repaired the bicycles ...

27. Die Lücken sollen ergänzt werden: „EACH OTHER" oder „ONE ANOTHER"!

a) Ann and Nelly are really not nice to ...

b) They got to know ... at the performance of that play.

c) The children should help ...

d) Ann and Sue are really very nice, they always help ...

e) The twins had their birthday, so they bought birthday presents for ...

28. Folgende Sätze sollen in die Mehrzahl gesetzt werden!

a) This is my purse, that is your purse.

b) This is our house, that is their house.

c) This is John's pet, that is Nelly's pet.

d) This is her room, that is John's room.

29. Folgende Sätze sollen sinngemäß wiedergegeben werden!

a) Heute morgen war es besonders kalt.

b) Damals war es möglich, heutzutage wäre so etwas unmöglich.

c) Die Kinder wollen ihre Englischkenntnisse verbessern, deshalb fahren sie jeden Sommer nach Brighton.

d) Er beendete sein Studium in dieser Woche.

e) Ich glaube, wir können jetzt aufhören. Das reicht.

30. Es soll nach jedem unterstrichenen Satzteil gefragt werden!

a) <u>Last winter</u> the <u>Coopers</u> went skiing <u>in Austria</u>.
     1   2   3

b) <u>Tom</u> spent his holidays <u>in Austria</u> because <u>he wanted to learn the German language</u>.
  1   2   3 / 4

c) <u>Mary</u> got <u>to the theatre</u> <u>by bus</u> <u>within a few minutes</u>.
   1   2   3   4

d) <u>Every summer</u> <u>Tom</u> travels <u>to New York</u>.
     1   2   3

e) Her new hat is green.
      1   2   3

f) Tom Smith is sixteen years old.
        1   2

g) Mr Cooper bought a new car for 5,000 £.
       1   2   3

31. Es soll jeweils das Fragefürwort ergänzt werden!

a) ... did you pay?

b) ... are you coming from?

c) ... are you looking for?

d) ... did the London train arrive?

e) ... did the guests stay?

f) ... wrote this book?

g) ... many people came to the fair?

h) ... do you like better, juice or Coke?

i) ... London's theatres are most popular?

j) ... scooter is this?

32. Folgende Sätze sollen auf Englisch wiedergegeben werden!

a) Welche Farbe hat dein neuer Pullover?

b) Was heißt „Grammatik" auf Englisch?

c) Wozu werden diese Schachteln hier gebraucht?

d) Wie alt ist unser Präsident?

e) Welche Farbe haben deine Lieblingsschuhe?

33. Das „Relativpronomen" soll jeweils ergänzt werden!

a) Here is the woman ... bought that expensive coat.

b) Mrs Miller's husband, ... is older than she is, is a professor.

c) The programme ... is on today is said to be amusing.

d) I want to offer him a book ... is not difficult to read.

e) Her eldest daughter, ... is very intelligent, is at the university.

f) Peter, ... sister you met, won the prize.

g) The gentleman, ... I wanted to help, had run short of petrol.

h) Here is the cat ... we gave some sausage.

i) Mrs Greene, ... husband is ill, can't come to our birthday party.

j) This is the poor dog ... master went on holiday.

k) Where are the boots ... I wore yesterday?

l) This is the comfortable armchair ... we bought yesterday.

34. Folgende Berufe sollen erklärt werden!

> A baker: A baker is a person who bakes bread, buns and rolls.

a) A shop-assistant
b) A joiner
c) A cook
d) A hairdresser
e) A playwright
f) A gardener

35. Der Verwendungszweck folgender Gegenstände soll erklärt werden!

> A hammer: A hammer is a tool which is used for driving nails into the wall.

a) A screwdriver
b) A pair of scissors
c) A knife
d) A camera
e) A needle
f) A typewriter

36. Folgende Sätze sollen vervollständigt werden!

> This is the most interesting building ... (to see)
> This is the most interesting building that I've ever seen.

a) This is the finest meal ... (to eat)

b) This is the best story ... (to read)

c) This is the most beautiful garden ... (to see)

d) This is the farthest journey ... (to make)

e) This is the most helpful book ... (to find)

37. *Folgende Sätze sollen sinngemäß wiedergegeben werden!*

a) Im Ausverkauf kauften sie alles, was billig war.

b) Die Bibel war das einzige Buch, das Mr Miller kannte.

c) Die ersten Engländer, die sich in Amerika niederließen, waren Puritaner.

d) Er erzählte mir etwas, was ich nicht vergessen kann.

e) Sie erzählten uns Dinge, die für uns sehr interessant waren.

f) Diese Weste hat genau die Farbe, die ich schon die ganze Zeit suche.

38. *Folgende Satzpaare sollen jeweils ohne Verwendung eines Relativpronomens verbunden werden.*

> This was the best play. I have seen it.
> This was the best play I've seen.

a) Alcohol is a drug. Many people can't do without it.

b) What's the title of the story? Dad is looking for it.

c) Where are all the photos? You wanted to show me them.

d) What age is the woman? You were telling me about her.

e) This is the mountain. I climbed it last summer.

39. *Die Lücken sollen ergänzt werden: „WHO", „WHICH", „THAT" oder „kein Relativpronomen"!*

a) This was the most delicious meal ... we had ever eaten.

b) Dad, ... is a very quiet person, lost his temper.

c) The man ... I met yesterday was Mr Blackwell.

d) Are these all the letters ... you have written?

e) This is the clever boy ... won the first prize.

f) The noise ... Mr Miller's children made was intolerable.

g) Sue bought everything ... was expensive.

h) Is that the photo ... you were laughing at?

i) What you need is a little salt, ... you can find in the sideboard.

j) There isn't much to report ... would enjoy you.

k) The man ... entered the room looked very sad.

l) Here are all the pictures ... you were laughing at.

40. *Folgende Sätze sollen mit „relativen Anknüpfungen" zu Ende geführt werden!*

a) This place reminds me of the time **when** ...

b) This is the park **where** ...

c) This is the reason **why** ...

d) Friday is the day ...

e) Give me an explanation ...

f) Here is the place ...

g) And that was certainly not the reason ...

h) Let's fix the date ...

i) Find the place in your books ...

j) Little Tommy can't understand the reason ...

41. *In folgenden „Minidialogen" soll „SOME" bzw. „ANY" ergänzt werden!*

a) Is there ... sugar left? – I'm afraid there isn't ... left.

b) Have you got ... interesting stamps for me? – I'm sure I have ...

c) Dad, please, give me ... money. – If I had ... , I'd give you ...

d) Oh, these fine apples! Have you got ... for me? – Of course, you may have ...

42. Folgende Sätze sollen auf Englisch wiedergegeben werden!

a) Ist da jemand an der Tür?

b) Da muß irgendjemand an der Tür sein!

c) Jemand fragte nach dir.

d) Es war nicht möglich, den Schlüssel irgendwo zu finden.

e) Ich bin sicher, daß wir den Schlüssel irgendwo in der Küche finden.

f) Irgendwie werden wir das Problem lösen. – Ich bin ganz sicher.

g) „Können wir noch irgend etwas für Sie tun?", fragte die Verkäuferin.

h) Wenn noch irgend etwas zu tun ist, kann ich dir helfen.

43. Die richtige Form (EVERY, EACH, ANY) soll jeweils eingesetzt werden!

a) ... vehicle must have a number plate.

b) ... boy here must study hard.

c) ... of these exercises is rather easy.

d) Joe is a very clever boy. He can answer ... question.

e) You may take ... of the bottles.

f) You may choose ... bracelet you like.

g) ... tree bears some fruit.

h) ... of these trees bore delicious apples last autumn.

i) ... player gets five cards.

j) ... article has been reduced by 20%.

k) ... of these articles has been reduced.

l) The children used to watch TV. ... night.

44. Folgende Sätze sollen auf Englisch wiedergegeben werden!

a) Die Freunde treffen einander jeden zweiten Tag.

b) Dann und wann gingen sie ins Theater.

c) Diese Pullover kosten je 10 £.

d) Alles muß bis Mittag fertig sein.

e) Er war beinahe überall.

45. Die richtige Form (ALL, WHOLE) soll jeweils eingesetzt werden!

a) ... children like chocolate.

b) The Coopers travelled round the ... of Scotland.

c) ... of them went skating last Sunday.

d) ... the guests brought nice presents.

e) He read the ... novel in one evening.

f) Tommy ate the ... cake.

46. Folgende Sätze sollen auf Englisch wiedergegeben werden!

a) Sie schauten sich den ganzen Tag Sehenswürdigkeiten an.

b) Im ganzen gesehen war es ein interessanter Film.

c) Sie streiten oft, aber trotzdem sind sie Freunde.

d) Sie spazierten durch den Wald, als – ganz plötzlich – ein Jäger aus dem Gebüsch auftauchte.

e) Als sie aus dem Kaufhaus kamen, hatten sie eine ganze Menge unnützer Dinge eingekauft.

47. Folgende Sätze sollen auf Englisch wiedergegeben werden!

a) Diese beiden Damen sind eifersüchtig.

b) Beide Mädchen werden im Sommer nach England fahren.

c) Keiner der beiden Studenten wird die Prüfung bestehen.

d) London liegt zu beiden Seiten der Themse.

e) Wer wird das Rennen gewinnen, John oder Fred? – Ich weiß nicht, jeder (von beiden) kann gewinnen.

48. *Folgende Sätze sollen auf Englisch wiedergegeben werden!*

a) Die Millers wohnen auf der anderen Seite der Straße.

b) Joe und Fred spielten Fußball, die anderen gingen radfahren.

c) Hättest du gern noch eine Tasse Tee?

d) Falls diese Jacke nicht paßt, probieren Sie bitte eine andere.

e) Jemand anderer wird Ihnen die Kathedrale zeigen.

f) Neulich trafen sie einander im Restaurant.

g) Ich hoffe, er wird doch einmal sein Studium beenden.

h) Ich würde Ihnen gern etwas anderes zeigen.

49. *Folgende Sätze sollen auf Englisch wiedergegeben werden!*

a) Frag niemanden.

b) Keine ihrer Freundinnen kam zu ihrer Geburtstagsparty.

c) Ich bin sicher, daß dir niemand helfen wird.

d) Hast du etwas gesehen? – Nein, nichts.

e) Das ist streng geheim. – Erzähl niemandem davon.

50. *Folgende Sätze sollen jeweils ergänzt werden!*
    ① *„MUCH" bzw. „MANY":*

a) There were not ... children at the party.

b) He hasn't got ... books.

c) There wasn't ... wine in Mr Miller's cellar.

d) " ... ado about nothing" is the title of a Shakespearian comedy.

e) How ... stamps did you buy?

② *„LITTLE" bzw. „(A) FEW":*

a) He bought ... bananas.

b) Mrs Miller earns very ... money.

c) The Coopers will come at four. I'll buy ... pieces of cake (ein paar).

d) Just take ... sugar (ein wenig).

e) They ate ... , but they drunk ... glasses of juice (ein paar).

51. *Die Lücken sollen ergänzt werden!*

a) When he was in the USA he earned ____ money.
   (viel)

b) Read this text ____ times.
   (viele)

c) ____ of tourists came to Mozart's birthplace.
   (Viele)

d) Hurry up, we've already lost ____ time.
   (viel)

e) ____ endurance will be necessary.
   (Viel)

THE ADJECTIVE

COMPARISON AND USE

a **big** boy – a **big** girl – a **big** house

a **beautiful** girl .... the girl is **beautiful**
a **clever** boy .... the boy is **clever**
a **new** book .... the book is **new**

This pencil is **long**. The green pencil is even **longer**.
The red pencil is **longest**.

Jim is a **clever** boy. Pat is **cleverer** than Jim.
Peter is **cleverest**.

Mr Miller is **polite**. Mr Brown is **politer** than Mr Miller.
Mr Smith is **politest**.

DAS EIGENSCHAFTSWORT (ADJEKTIV)

1. STEIGERUNG UND ANWENDUNG

Das **Adjektiv** kennzeichnet die **Eigenschaft** einer Person oder Sache, die durch ein **Substantiv** bezeichnet ist.

Das **Adjektiv** ist in Geschlecht, Zahl und Fall **unveränderlich (flektiert nicht).**

Das **Adjektiv** kann

- **Attribut** zu einem Substantiv sein
- **Prädikatsnomen** sein, Teil der Satzaussage

Die Steigerung

- „German Comparison": ähnlich wie im Deutschen auf -er, -est

  ● alle einsilbig gesprochenen Adjektiva

Positiv	Komparativ	Superlativ
long	– longer	– longest
short	– shorter	– shortest

  ● zweisilbige Adjektiva mit folgenden Endungen: -y, -le, -er, -ow

happy	– happier	– happiest
noble	– nobler	– noblest
clever	– cleverer	– cleverest
narrow	– narrower	– narrowest

  ● zweisilbige Adjektiva mit der Betonung auf der letzten Silbe

polite	– politer	– politest
sincere	– sincerer	– sincerest

  ebenso: pleasent, solid, stupid, civil, common, cruel
  quiet

The cartoons were **interesting**. The news were **more interesting**. The documentary was **most interesting**.

Peter is **cautious**. Ann is **more cautious**.
Jimmy is **most cautious**.

Even the **stupidest** pupil must be able to understand these rules.
That was one of the **most stupid** mistakes he has ever made.

Betty's answer was really **good**. Jane's answer was **better**. Mary's answer was **best**.

Are you **well**? No, it could be **better**.

He showed **little** interest in our slides.
The Blackwells showed even **less** interest.

Tom is a **little** boy.
Jim is even **smaller**.

– **„French Comparison"**: ähnlich wie im Französischen; Steigerung erfolgt mit „more" und „most" (vgl. lat. magis idoneus, maxime idoneus)

● alle drei- und mehrsilbigen Adjektiva

beautiful	– more beautiful	– most beautiful
interesting	– more interesting	– most interesting

● zweisilbige Adjektiva mit Anfangsbetonung

terrible	– more terrible	– most terrible
splendid	– more splendid	– most splendid

ebenso: famous, active, cautious, careful, useless, ...

Beachte!

Es gibt im Englischen <u>keine starren Regeln</u> für die Steigerung.

Sprachrhythmus und Wohlklang der Sprache sind ausschlaggebend für die eine oder andere Form der Steigerung.

Unregelmäßige Steigerung:

good	(gut)		
well	(wohl, gesund)	– better	– best
bad	(schlecht)		
ill	(krank)	– worse	– worst
evil	(böse)		
much	(viel)		
many	(viele)	– more	– most
little	(wenig)	– less	– least
	(klein)	– smaller	– smallest

Where is the **nearest** post office? The **nearest** post office is closed; you must go to the **next** post office.
The **next** day they posted the letter.

I'll come to see you later. Here are the **latest** news (there will be more).
Here are Jim and Joe. The **latter** will do the shopping. (der letztere)
The **last** news (there will be no more).

Paris is **farther** from Vienna than Rome.
Let's wait for **further** news. (weitere)

Jim is **older** than Tom.
Jim is my **elder** brother.

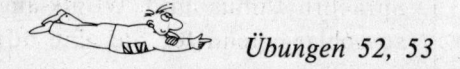

Übungen 52, 53

The quality of this fur is **inferior** to that.
Mr Brown was **senior to** all the other applicants, that's why he got the professorship.

The most important court in the USA is the **Supreme Court.**

Doppelformen im Komparativ und Superlativ:

near
- nearer – nearest (Entfernung)
- – – next (Reihenfolge)

late
- later – latest (Zeit)
- latter – last (Reihenfolge)

far
- farther – farthest (Entfernung)
- further – furthest (Aufzählung)

old
- older – oldest (in Vergleichssätzen)
- elder – eldest (beifügend, in Aussagen über Familienmitglieder)

Steigerungsformen ohne Positiv:

Einige Adjektiva besitzen nur die Form des Komparativs oder Superlativs

inferior to	niedriger, geringer als
superior to	höher, überlegen
major	größer, wichtiger
minor	kleiner, geringer
senior to	älter als, ranghöher
junior to	jünger als, untergeordnet
extreme	äußerst
supreme	höchst, oberst

Tom is ⬚as⬚ tall ⬚as⬚ Peter.

Peter is ⬚not so⬚ clever ⬚as⬚ Tom.
Tom is ⬚not as⬚ intelligent ⬚as⬚ Pat.

Pat is <u>more intelligent</u> than Tom.

Looking down from the plane he said, "The houses are growing **smaller and smaller**."
This book is becoming **more and more interesting**.

He is **very nice** and a **most handsome** young man.

This film is **much more interesting** than Fellini's films.
Today he is **even more diligent** than yesterday.
She is **far better** at arithmetic than at geometry.

Your last test was <u>better</u> **by far**.

He was **by far** the **most learned** professor.
He was the **most learned** professor **of all**.

The more I know about her, **the better** I like her.

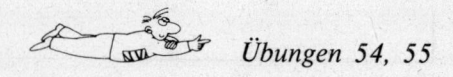

Übungen 54, 55

Beachte!

- die **Steigerungsformen in Vergleichssätzen**

    ● **Gleichheit** wird ausgedrückt

    $\boxed{\text{AS}}$ – POSITIV – $\boxed{\text{AS}}$ ... so ... wie

Verneint:

$\boxed{\text{NOT SO}}$
$\boxed{\text{NOT AS}}$ – POSITIV – $\boxed{\text{AS}}$ ... nicht so ... wie

    ● **Ungleichheit** wird ausgedrückt

    KOMPARATIV + THAN   ... -er ... als

- die **allmähliche Steigerung**

    „IMMER" + KOMPARATIV

- die **Verstärkung der Steigerungsformen**

    ● **Positiv:** verstärkt durch „very" (sehr), „most" (überaus)

    ● **Komparativ:** verstärkt durch „much" (viel), „even" (sogar noch), „still" (noch), „far" (weit)

Anmerkung!

„By far" (bei weitem) steht immer hinter dem Komparativ.

    ● **Superlativ:** verstärkt durch „by far" (bei weitem), „... of all" (the greatest of all ... der allergrößte ...)

- die Wendung „THE + KOMPARATIV, THE + KOMPARATIV" (je ... desto)

Tom's **elder** brother moved to London in 1980.
He is five years **older** than Tom.

Skiing is my **favourite** sport.
I like skiing **best of all**.

I like **wooden** toys best of all.
This little doll is **made of wood**.

Put on your **woollen** stockings.
These stockings are **made of wool**.

Before you sign the paper read the **above** remark.
The post office is in an **off** street of Oxford Street.

This **silk** scarf was a bargain.
She must wash her **silken** hair with a special shampoo.

Übung 56

Gebrauch des Adjektivs:

- **ATTRIBUTIV**

... einige Adjektiva werden ausschließlich attributiv gebraucht:

elder

favourite

wooden

woollen

Beachte die Verwendung anderer Wortarten als attributive Adjektive:

the **above** remark	die obige Bemerkung
an **off** street	eine Seitenstraße
an **up** train	ein n a c h London fahrender Zug

a silver coin
paper money
London Bridge
a March wind
April showers

a silk scarf
BUT: silken hair   seidiges Haar

a gold watch
BUT: the golden age   das Goldene Zeitalter

It was an extremely **warm** day.

A tower 150 feet **high** was to be seen from all over the district.

It was a problem **too difficult** for us.

He is **quick**.
She became **angry**.
It's getting **bright**.

He stood **white** with fear.
The bus left the station **empty**.
They landed **safe** and **sound**.

They all considered his decision **correct**.
He was found **guilty** after all.

Tom and Fred look **alike**.
Joe had a **similar** idea.

Beachte die Stellung des attributiv gebrauchten Adjektivs!

VOR dem zugehörigen Substantiv

NACH dem Substantiv

- wenn das Adjektiv durch Maß- und Zahlenangaben erweitert ist
- in Verbindung mit „as", „so", „too" zur Hervorhebung
- in einigen Redewendungen

the best way imaginable	der bestvorstellbare Weg
from time immemorial	seit uralten Zeiten

- **PRÄDIKATIV**

- als Ergänzung zum Subjekt

  - nach Verben des Seins, Werdens: to be, to become, to get, to grow ...

  - nach Verben der Ruhe und der Bewegung: to stand, to sit, to lie, to remain, to leave, to return ...

- als Ergänzung zum Objekt

  - nach Verben des Dafürhaltens und Erklärens: to consider, to call, to find ...

Beachte folgende Adjektiva!

Nur prädikativ gebraucht werden	Bedeutung	Attributive Entsprechung
alike	gleich, ähnlich	similar, equal

Baby is **asleep**.
Leave a **sleeping** dog alone.

Christopher Columbus was **aware** of the dangers.
You should keep a **watchful** eye on that dog.

This old coin is **worth** a lot.
"Turn again Whittington, thou **worthy** citizen of London."

The wind was **still,** so the surfers had to swim back.
Look at the **calm** sea! We can't go sailing today.

Übung 57

Always expect **the worst**.
Don't try **the impossible**.

A lot of organisations try to help **the poor** and **the sick**.

A **blind** man was one of the best telephone operators.

The Austrians are very proud of their lakes and mountains.
The French and **the Dutch** live on the Continent, **the English** don't.
"**The Flying Dutchman**" is an interesting opera by Richard Wagner.
The Swiss are famous for their watches.
Look, a **Chinese**! – No, it's a **Japanese**.

Übung 58

alive	am Leben	live
alone	allein, einsam	lonely
asleep	eingeschlafen, schlafend	sleeping
awake	wach	waking
aware of	gewahr	watchful
content	zufrieden	contented
ill	krank	sick
well	gesund, wohl	healthy
worth	wert	worthy (würdig)
still	ruhig	calm

- **SUBSTANTIVISCH**

Durch **Vorsetzen des bestimmten Artikels** wird das **Adjektiv** – wie im Deutschen – zum **Substantiv** und bezeichnet

- einen abstrakten Begriff

- die Gesamtheit von Personen mit gleicher Eigenschaft

Beachte!

Wird nur eine Person aus dieser Gesamtheit gemeint, wird „man, woman, lady, ..." hinzugefügt.

- die Zugehörigkeit zu einem Volk

Beachte Singular und Plural der Völkernamen auf „-sh" und „-ch"

the English – an Englishman
the French – a Frenchman
the Dutch – a Dutchman

Völkernamen auf „-se" und „-ss" haben für **Singular** und **Plural** dieselbe Form.

Mr Visconti is an **Italian**.
The **Italians** know how to produce fashionable shoes.

The Republicans and **the Democrats** want to win the election.
The **natives** of New Zealand are called Aborigines.

PARTICULAR ADJECTIVES

She was **furious at** Nelly's bad manners.
G. B. Shaw is **famous for** his comedies.

Mr Miller's garden was not **safe from** the wild animals in spite of the fence.
During the nineteenth century Newcastle was **abundant in** coal.

Mr Brown was **tired of** working in the garden.
Welcome to our new house.

Tom fell **ill with** the measles.

Übung 59

Völkernamen auf „-an" und „-on" bilden **Pluralformen** wie Substantive.
- das Mitglied einer politischen Partei oder Religionsgemeinschaft

  a Conservative   a Democrat
  a Liberal   a Catholic
  a Republican   a Protestant

  ebenso: a black, a white, a saint, a native ...

2. BESONDERHEITEN DER ADJEKTIVA

Adjektiva mit Präpositionen

Adjective + AT

furious at	wütend über
happy at	glücklich über

Adjective + FOR

anxious for	begierig auf
famous for	berühmt wegen
remarkable for	bemerkenswert wegen

Adjective + FROM

different from	verschieden von
far from	weit (entfernt) von
free from	frei von
safe from	sicher vor

Adjective + IN

abundant in	(über)reich an
poor in	arm an
rich in	reich an

Adjective + OF

characteristic of	bezeichnend für
conscious of	bewußt
envious of	neidisch auf
jealous of	eifersüchtig auf
proud of	stolz auf
sure of	sicher
tired of	überdrüssig, müde
typical of	typisch für

Adjective + TO

attentive to	aufmerksam auf
cruel to	grausam gegen
equal to	gleich
grateful to	dankbar für
helpful to	hilfreich
indifferent to	gleichgültig gegen
kind to	freundlich zu
similar to	ähnlich
welcome to	willkommen

Adjective + WITH

ill with / sick with	krank an

It's fashionable to wear a **broad** belt.
Mr Smith is a **broad**-shouldered man.

This carpet is 10 feet long and 8 feet **wide**.
The pioneers crossed the **wide** plains.

Übung 60

Joe is really too **stupid**. He can't understand these theories.

It was rather boring, there were only **dull** people there.

She's a **silly** girl, but she's gifted for tennis and basket-ball.

Look at Pat! He's too **clumsy** to hold the spade.

It was **foolish** of him to tell such lies.

It was **unwise** of her to sell her flat before she had found another.

Übung 61 ①

Besonderheiten im Gebrauch

BREIT, WEIT

- **broad:** Gegensatz zu „narrow"

in broad daylight	am hellichten Tage
a broad joke	ein derber Witz
in the broadest sense	im weitesten Sinne
it is as broad as it is long	gehüpft wie gesprungen
a broad accent	ein breiter Akzent

- **wide:** Gegensatz zu „small"

a wide public	ein breites Publikum
the wide world	die weite Welt
far and wide	weit und breit

DUMM

- **stupid:** „schwerfällig im Denken"
- **dull:** „schwerfällig, langweilig"
- **silly:** „albern"
- **clumsy:** „unbeholfen, ungeschickt"
- **foolish:** „töricht"

  foolproof — narrensicher

- **unwise:** „unklug"

Beachte!

sich **dumm** stellen	to play the fool
Das ist zu **dumm**!	How awkward!
der **Dumme** sein	to be the loser
Sei nicht so **dumm**!	Be your age!

What's the matter with him? He looked **serious** this morning.
Can't you ever be **serious**?

I'm sure you'll pass the exam, if you study **earnestly**.
"The Importance Of Being **Earnest**" was written by Oscar Wilde.

I expect this play to be **grave**, it's a drama.

Übung 61 ②

I don't feel well in that hotel, it's so **strange**.
They found shelter in a **strange** old inn.

I suppose her to be French, she has a **foreign** accent.

There were a lot of **exotic** plants in the glass house.

Übung 62

Isn't Joe **clever**? He has repaired his radio.
You should read this book. It's rather **clever**.

Only the most **intelligent** students passed all the exams.

ERNST

- **serious:** ernst zu nehmen

to take something seriously	etwas ernst nehmen
a serious rival	ein ernster Rivale

- **earnest:** „nachdenklich, strebsam, gewissenhaft"

- **grave:** „gesetzt, bedenklich"

FREMD

- **strange:** „fremdartig, neu, unbekannt"

- **foreign:** „ausländisch"

foreign languages	Fremdsprachen
foreign affairs	auswertige Angelegenheiten
foreign trade	Außenhandel

- **exotic:** ... von Pflanzen ...

Beachte!

fremde Hilfe	outside help
in **fremden** Händen	in other hands
unter **fremdem** Namen	under an assumed name, incognito
ich bin hier **fremd**	I'm a stranger here

GESCHEIT

- **clever:** „geschickt, gewandt, geistreich"

- **intelligent:** „von rascher Auffassung, vernunftbegabt, gebildet"

Little Tommy is a **bright** boy.

It was a **wise** decision.
It's **wiser** to go home.

Betty is a **sensible** little girl.

Übung 63 ①

The concert took place in the **great** hall.
Shaw was a **great** dramatist.
A **great** number of fans came to the festival.

The Browns have a **large** garden near Brighton.
There are **large** plains in Burgenland.

The Coopers have three **big** boys.
The Smiths bought a **big** house in Newham.

There are **huge forests** in Canada.
The Statue of Liberty, a **huge** woman, was one of the first items on our sightseeing programme.

- **bright:** „aufgeweckt"

- **wise:** „weise, vernünftig, erfahren, einsichtig"

    to be none the wiser   nicht klüger sein als zuvor

- **sensible:** „vernünftig"

Beachte!

Sei doch **gescheit!**   Don't be a fool!
                                    Do be sensible!

Daraus werde ich nicht   I can't make head
gescheit.   or tail of it

GROSS

- **great:** „umfangreich", bezogen auf Ausdehnung, Dauer

    a great many   sehr viele
    to a great extent   in hohem Maße

- **large:** „ausgedehnt"

    large as life   in Lebensgröße
    a large sum   eine beträchtliche Summe
    a large income   hohes Einkommen

- **big:** „groß und breit", weit verbreitet im „Spoken English"

    the big toe   die große Zehe
    a big voice   eine volle Stimme
    big game   Großwild

- **huge:** „riesig, sehr groß"

Mary is rather **tall** for her age.
The steeple of our little church is rather **tall**.
There were **tall** cypress-trees on either side of the road.

We had a **grand** dinner.
Let's travel to Sicily. – That's a **grand** idea.

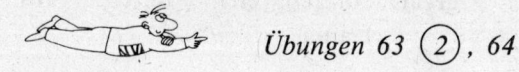

Übungen 63 ②, 64

It was a **good** idea to get these tickets.
"Right", said the teacher.
Our neighbours are very **kind** people.
Santa Claus is a **kind** old man.
Our barber's apprentice is a **capable** young man.
When the weather is **fine** we can go boating.
Try the long knife, it's **useful**.

- **tall:** „groß (von Wuchs)" ..., Menschen, Bäume, Türme, ...

that's a tall order	das ist ein bißchen viel verlangt
to talk tall	prahlen

- **grand:** „groß(artig)"

to have grand time	sich köstlich amüsieren

Beachte!

ein **großer** Fehler	a bad mistake
ein **großer** Verlust	a heavy loss
ein **großer** Buchstabe	a capital letter
großschreiben	to capitalize
große Ferien	long vacations
große Terz	major third
große Toilette	full dress
ich bin kein **großer** Tänzer	I'm not much of a dancer
großjährig sein	to be of age
im **großen** und ganzen	on the whole

GUT

- **good:** (allgemein)
- **right:** „richtig"
- **kind:** „gutherzig, gutmütig"
  will you be so kind as to ...   sei so gut ...
- **capable:** „tüchtig"
- **fine:** „fein, prächtig"
- **useful:** „nützlich"

Beachte!

gute Nerven	steady nerves
gute Qualität	high (good) quality
auf **gut** deutsch	in plain English

Übung 65 (1)

He took **little** trouble with his work.
He took **little** interest in my photos.

Sue is taking her **little** dog for a walk.
The Cooper twins are two pretty **little** girls.

Wait **a little**!
Some more sugar, Betty? – Just **a little**.

Austria is **smaller** than Britain.

A small person is **short** and slim.
Baden is but a **short** distance from Vienna.
The director held a **short** speech.

Übung 65 (2)

zu **guter** Letzt	finally
gut sein mit jemandem	to be on friendly terms with ...
Mach's **gut**!	good luck
Schon **gut**!	never mind
Laß es **gut** sein!	let it be

KLEIN

- **little**: nur attributiv gebraucht

  ● „klein, unbedeutend, wenig"

  ● entspricht unserem „-chen, -lein", gefühlsbetont

a little	ein bißchen

- **small**: „klein, schmächtig", Anzahl, Ausdehnung

a small voice	eine leise Stimme
the small change	Kleingeld
small letters	Kleinbuchstaben
on a small scale	im kleinen

- **short**: „kurz (von Wuchs)" ... Entfernung, Zeit

Beachte!

kleine Terz	minor third
im **kleinen** verkaufen	to sell by detail

Let's have a **light** meal today.
What about some **light** wine?
It's warm today, I'll take my **light** jacket.
I like **light** music, such as operettas and musicals.

The mathematics test was **easy**.

A **gentle** breeze was blowing.

Übung 66

Ann loves singing, dancing, and **merry** parties.
"A **Merry** Christmas" to all of you.

Mrs Brown bought some **gay** curtains and **gay** cushions for her sitting-room.

The twins are really **cheerful**.

Did you see this **funny** film?

The party was **amusing**, indeed.

Übung 67 ①

I caught a **bad** cold.

What a **wicked** little person she is!

You will be punished for your **evil** deeds.

LEICHT

- **light:** ... Essen, Wein, Kleidung, Musik ...
  with a light heart leichten Herzens

- **easy:** „mühelos, einfach"
  to take it easy sich Zeit lassen, es sich gemütlich machen
  that was no easy job das war nicht leicht
  easy of access leicht zugänglich

- **gentle:** „sanft"

Beachte!
leicht entzündlich highly inflammable
leicht löslich readily soluble

LUSTIG

- **merry:** „fröhlich"

- **gay:** „fröhlich, munter, bunt"

- **cheerful:** „heiter (von Natur aus), vergnügt"

- **funny:** „komisch, drollig"

- **amusing:** „belustigend"

SCHLECHT

- **bad:** (allgemein)

- **wicked:** „boshaft, verschlagen"

- **evil:** „böse"

What he said was really **base**.

Übung 67 (2)

Look at these **beautiful** flowers!
What a **beautiful** garden!
"My **Fair** Lady" is a famous musical by Frederick Loewe.

Mr Harrison is a **handsome** young man.
What a **pretty** girl she is!

Lovely day today, isn't it?
The weather was **fine**, so we went boating every day.

Übungen 68, 69 (1)

– **base**: „gemein, niederträchtig"

Beachte!

schlechte Aussichten	poor prospects
schlechte Laune	ill humour
	bad temper
schlechte Zeiten	hard times

SCHÖN

– **beautiful**: (allgemein)

– **fair**: von Frauen

a fair sum	eine schöne Summe
fair words	schöne Worte

– **handsome, good-looking**: von Männern

– **pretty, nice**: „hübsch, nett"

a nice mess	eine schöne Bescherung

– **lovely**: „entzückend"

– **fine**: „gut, fein"

that's fine	das ist schön
a fine excuse	eine hübsche Ausrede
the fine arts	die schönen Künste
one fine morning	eines schönen Morgens

Beachte!

in **schönster** Ordnung	in apple-pie order
schönen Dank	many thanks
das ist **schön** von ihm	that's (very) kind of him
es war sehr **schön**	we had a good time
du bist mir ein **schöner** Freund	a fine friend you are

We couldn't carry the suitcase, it was too **heavy**.

The translation of this letter was rather **difficult**.

It was **hard** work to dig the garden.
The students worked **hard** for the exam.

BUT: John **hardly** worked.

He caught a **bad** cold.

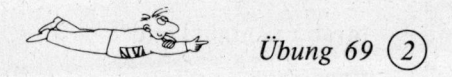

Übung 69 ②

SCHWER

- **heavy**: Gewicht

a heavy eater	ein starker Esser
a heavy loss	ein schwerer Verlust
heavy rain	starker, heftiger Regen

- **difficult**: „schwierig"

- **hard**: „schwierig, hart"

Achtung! hardly = kaum

- **bad**: „schlimm, böse"

schwerer Wein	strong wine
schwer von Begriff	slow (in the uptake)
schwer beleidigen	to offend deeply
schwer hören	to be hard of hearing
schwer enttäuscht	to be cruelly disappointed
schwer verwundet	dangerously wounded

ÜBUNGEN

52. Es sollen jeweils die beiden fehlenden Formen des Adjektivs ergänzt werden!

> good – better – best

long, happier, most useful, more careful, useless, well, worse, most, smallest, latter, furthest, farther, elder, oldest, ...

53. Die richtige Form der angegebenen Wörter soll ergänzt werden!

a) NEAR: The ... post office is off Regent Street. If it is closed, go to the ... post office.

What will you do ... holidays?

Who is the ... person to enter?

b) LATE: Have you heard the ... news?

We met the Millers ... summer in Venice.

All the girls arrived ... than I.

Here are Jim and Joe. – The former is my cousin, the ... is my brother.

She bought the ... fashion of Cerruti's.

c) FAR: London is ... from Vienna than Rome.

I'm rather interested in this election – let's wait for ... news.

She will need no ... help.

d) OLD: Peter is ... than his brother. He is his ... brother.

This here is the ... picture in the museum.

Old Jim is the ... member of family.

54. *Es sollen Vergleichssätze nach folgendem Muster gebildet werden!*

> strong: beer, wine, gin
>
> Beer is strong.
> Wine is stronger than beer.
> Gin is strongest.

a) high: Ben Nevis, the Großglockner, the Kilimanjaro
b) fast: scooter, car, aeroplane
c) big: pig, bull, elephant
d) expensive: silver, gold, platinum
e) beautiful: Miss Austria, Miss Europe, Miss World

55. *Der vollständige Satz soll auf Englisch wiedergegeben werden!*

a) He made a ball of snow and rolled it until it became _____.
   (immer größer)
b) Today the Millers are _____ than yesterday.
   (sogar noch freundlicher)
c) This story is becoming _____.
   (immer interessanter)
d) This house is becoming _____.
   (immer höher)
e) She is _____ and a _____ lady.
   (sehr charmant) (überaus intelligente)
f) Jane is _____ student at the academy.
   (bei weitem die fleißigste)
g) He was _____.
   (der allergrößte Schauspieler)
h) Look, this flower-bed is becoming _____.
   (immer schöner)
i) Tom is _____ at chemistry than at physics.
   (weitaus besser)
j) These novels are _____.
   (überaus bemerkenswert)
k) Her second book is _____.
   (sogar noch interessanter)
l) _____ I meet her, _____ I like her.
   (Je öfter) (um so weniger)

56. *Folgende Sätze sollen auf Englisch wiedergegeben werden!*

a) Tennis ist mein Lieblingssport. Ich mag Tennis am liebsten.

b) Peters älterer Bruder kam aus Amerika zurück. – Er ist zwei Jahre älter als Peter.

c) Diese Fäustlinge hier sind nicht aus Wolle. – Zieh dir deine Wollfäustlinge an!

d) Viele Kinder haben Holzspielzeug gerne. Diese kleine Spielzeugeisenbahn ist aus Holz.

e) Diese Seidenbluse war ein Gelegenheitskauf.

f) Ihr seidiges Haar wurde von vielen bewundert.

57. *Folgende Sätze sollen auf Englisch wiedergegeben werden!*

a) Ann and Sue are twins. They look _____ .
   (ähnlich)

b) The neighbours left Mrs Hoover quite _____ .
   (allein)

c) Don't disturb! Dad's _____ .
   (eingeschlafen)

d) A proverb says: Early to bed and early to rise makes a man _____ and wealthy and wise.
   (gesund)

e) You may enter. Dad's _____ .
   (wach)

f) "_____ boy" is the title of a famous song.
   (Einsam)

g) His stamps are _____ a lot.
   (wert)

h) Look at the _____ lake. We can't go surfing today.
   (ruhig)

i) Keep a _____ eye on these animals.
   (wachsam)

j) His _____ smile is known all over the country.
   (zufrieden)

k) The wind is _____ . – Let's have a swim today.
   (ruhig)

l) All the people were _____ with this solution.
   (zufrieden)

58. Es sollen Sätze nach folgendem Muster in der Einzahl gebildet werden!

> The Austrians:
> An Austrian speaks German.

The Dutch, the French, the Swiss, the Chinese, the English, the Irish, . . .

59. *Folgende Sätze sollen auf Englisch wiedergegeben werden!*
a) Die Alpen in Österreich sind arm an Gold und Silber.
b) Diese Worte sind bezeichnend für ihre schlechten Manieren.
c) Die gotische Kathedrale ist berühmt wegen ihres hohen Turmes.
d) Sie war glücklich über seine Ankunft.
e) Dieser Wein ist typisch für diese Gegend.
f) Du solltest zu deinen Nachbarn freundlich sein.
g) Im letzten Februar erkrankten viele Kinder an Grippe.

60. *Folgende Sätze sollen sinngemäß wiedergegeben werden!*
a) Der Mörder griff seine Opfer am hellichten Tag an.
b) Diesen Witz solltest du nicht in der Schule erzählen; das ist ein derber Witz.
c) Aufgrund ihres breiten Akzents hörten wir sofort, daß sie aus Manchester kam.
d) Ein breites Publikum besuchte die Ausstellung.
e) Auf dieser Ausstellung war die weite Welt zu bewundern.

61. *Das treffende Wort soll jeweils eingesetzt werden!*

① DUMM:
a) He is too . . . to cut his bread.
b) It was . . . of her to tell such nonsense.
c) Stop this nonsense. Don't be so . . .
d) Slow Joe doesn't see the joke, he's too . . .
e) Pat is too . . . He'll never be able to understand these rules.
f) It was really . . . of him to sell his car before he had bought another.

② ERNST:

a) This person is a ... rival.

b) You should study ..., if you intend to take the exam next week.

c) I expect the second part of this symphony to be ...

d) We should take this matter ...

62. *Folgende Sätze sollen auf Englisch wiedergegeben werden!*

a) Diese Firma ist schon seit jeher in fremden Händen.
b) Können Sie mir sagen, wo das Rathaus ist? – Ich bin fremd hier.
c) Sie ist zu stolz, als daß sie um fremde Hilfe ersuchen würde.
d) Ich bin überzeugt, daß sie nicht aus England kommt; sie hat einen fremden Akzent.

63. *Das treffende Wort soll jeweils eingesetzt werden!*

① GESCHEIT:

a) Isn't the farmer ... ? He's repaired the combiner.

b) Only the most ... pupils were allowed to take their final exams.

c) Baby is only 6 months old, but she's rather ...

d) It was a ... decision to stop this interview.

e) Don't disturb Dad now! Be a ... girl.

② GROSS:

a) The play was performed in the ... auditorium.

b) There are ... plains in Hungary.

c) Mr Miller has bought a ... car, a Mercedes.

d) Tommy is very ... for his age.

e) Let's go to the pictures. – That's a ... idea (großartig).

f) The memorial of Christopher Columbus, a ... column, is to be seen all over the harbor.

g) She has broken her ... toe.

64. Folgende Sätze sollen auf Englisch wiedergegeben werden!

a) Sehr viele Leute besuchten die Ausstellung.

b) Dieser Sänger ist für seine volle Stimme bekannt.

c) Sie wollte, daß wir den Rasen mähen; aber das war ein bißchen viel verlangt.

d) Es tut mir leid, ich bin kein großer Tänzer.

e) Du solltest alle diese Überschriften groß schreiben.

f) Sein Tod war ein großer Verlust.

g) Er machte einen großen Fehler; aus diesem Grund bekam er den Posten nicht!

h) In Österreich beginnen die großen Ferien im Juli.

65. Das treffende Wort soll jeweils eingesetzt werden!

① GUT:

a) If the weather were ..., we could go swimming.

b) Will you be so ... as to help me with my exercise?

c) Fred is really a ... student (tüchtig).

d) "...", said the teacher and Joe sat down.

e) I'm sure he'll have a ... idea.

f) If I were you, I'd take this costume, it's ... quality.

g) If you want to become a teacher, you need ... nerves.

h) "... luck!", he said and went off.

② KLEIN:

a) Windsor is but a ... distance from London.

b) Austria is ... than Italy.

c) The Hoovers took ... interest in our slides.

d) You should play the ... third.

e) Mrs Blackwell is ... and slim.

f) Pat is taking his ... sister for a walk.

66. *Folgende Sätze sollen auf Englisch wiedergegeben werden!*

a) Leichten Herzens verließen sie das Gerichtsgebäude.

b) Diese Höhle ist nicht leicht zugänglich.

c) Heute ist es warm. Ich werde den leichten Mantel anziehen.

d) Das ist nicht einfach, diese Farben sind leicht entzündlich.

e) Ein leichtes Lüftchen wehte, und wir konnten surfen gehen.

67. *Der treffende Ausdruck soll jeweils eingesetzt werden!*

① LUSTIG:

a) This film was rather ...

b) The Blackwell children are always ...

c) Mrs Smith is famous for her ... hats.

d) I got to know him at one of Joe's ... birthday parties.

e) The children watched the ... little rabbits.

② SCHLECHT:

a) The thief was punished for his ... deeds.

b) When I met him he was in a ... temper.

c) War broke out and ... times were to begin.

d) What he called his brother was ...

e) Beware Mrs Miller! She's a ... person.

68. *Folgende Sätze sollen auf Englisch wiedergegeben werden!*

a) Alles ist in schönster Ordnung, schönen Dank!

b) Das ist eine hübsche Ausrede – du bist mir ein schöner Freund.

c) Eines schönen Morgens trafen sie die Coopers.

d) Das ist sehr schön von ihr, aber ich glaube, das sind nur schöne Worte.

e) Schönes Wetter heute, nicht war?

69. Der treffende Ausdruck soll jeweils eingesetzt werden!

① SCHÖN:

a) When they married, Mrs Brown was a . . . young lady, Mr Brown was a . . . young gentleman.

b) A . . . mess you've left behind!

c) Young Mrs Miller is a . . . girl.

d) The weather is . . . today.

e) She was delighted with the . . . flowers.

② SCHWER:

a) The porter couldn't lift the suitcase, it was too . . .

b) It was . . . work to type this manuscript.

c) The last maths test was too . . . for most of the children.

d) Mrs Brown took a walk in the rain and caught a . . . cold.

e) Many of the soldiers were . . . wounded.

THE ADVERB

quick   – quickly
noble   – nobly (Endsilbe „-le" fällt weg)
full   – fully
wonderful – wonderfully
happy   – happily („y" wird zu „i")

Joe is a **friendly** boy. He always greets us **in a friendly way**.

surprising – surprisingly

excited   – excitedly

He always reads "The **Daily** Mail".
He reads this newspaper **daily**.

The **early** bird catches the worm.
They get up **early**.

This is the **best** book I've ever read.
I like this one **best**, too.

DAS UMSTANDSWORT (ADVERB)

Das **Adverb** dient zur **näheren** Bestimmung eines Wortes oder eines **ganzen Satzes**.

Man unterscheidet:

- **ursprüngliche Adverbien:** here, there, now, then, often, early, very, quite, ...

- durch **Zusammensetzung** gebildete **Adverbien:** always, already, today, tomorrow, ...

- **abgeleitete Adverbien:** slowly, quickly, beautifully, ...

Bildung der abgeleiteten Adverbien:

- aus einem **Adjektiv** durch Anhängen der Nachsilbe „-ly"

Beachte!

Adjektiva, die bereits auf „ly" enden, werden umschrieben.
friendly – in a friendly way
lively   – in a lively manner

- aus einem „Present Participle"

- aus einem „Past Participle"

Beachte!

Einige **Adjektiva** und **Adverbien** haben

- gleiche Form und **gleiche** Bedeutung: daily, early, hourly, weekly, ... better, best, less, least, last, worse, worst, ...

His **only** friend had an accident.
It happened **only** two hours ago.

Sue is a **pretty** girl.
Yesterday we were **pretty** excited.

How are you today? – **Well**, thanks.
"**Well** done!" said the teacher distributing the tests.

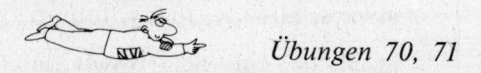

Übungen 70, 71

Pat worked **hard**.
Joe **hardly** worked.

These curtains sell **dear**.
He loves her **dearly**.

Our team played **fair**.
Jim and Joe played **fairly** well.

She held the baby **close**.
They were **closely** connected.

Übung 72

Tom skied **fast**.
Jim skied **faster**.
Mary skied **fastest**.

Sue did her exercise **carefully**.
Ann did it **more carefully**.
Betty did her exercise **most carefully**.

Übung 73

- gleiche Form und **unterschiedliche** Bedeutung

Gleiche Form	Bedeutung	
	als Adjektiv	als Adverb
ONLY	einzig	nur
PRETTY	hübsch	ziemlich
STILL	still	noch (immer)
WELL	wohl	gut

Einige Adjektiva besitzen zwei Formen mit unterschiedlicher Bedeutung:

hard (schwer)   – hardly (kaum)
near (nahe)   – nearly (fast, beinahe)
late (spät)   – lately (neulich, unlängst)
dear (teuer)   – dearly (lieb, zärtlich)
fair (fair, ehrlich)   – fairly (ziemlich)
close (fest, eng an sich gedrückt)   – closely (eng, intim)

Die Steigerung der Adverbien:

- **Einsilbige Adverbien** steigern auf „-er", „-est"
  fast – faster – fastest
  hard – harder – hardest

- **Mehrsilbige (abgeleitete) Adverbien** steigern mit „more" und „most"
  quickly   – more quickly   – most quickly
  beautifully – more beautifully – most beautifully

- **Unregelmäßige Steigerung:**
  well   – better – best
  badly – worse – worst

The children **very often** play the piano.
She **very seldom** goes to the pictures.

I'll wait **no** longer.
I can't wait **any** longer.

Mary <u>sings</u> **beautifully**.
     ↑
   Verb

Pat is **very** <u>slow</u>.
      ↑
   Adjektiv

Joe writes **very** <u>carefully</u>.
         ↑
     Adverb

Pat can't win the competition. He is **only** <u>a beginner</u>.
                                              ↑
                                            Substantiv

There we are.
Yesterday we were **here**.
Soon we'll be there.

He **often** reads books in the evening.
I **always** do my work in the afternoon.
Have you **ever** heard such an interesting story?
I have **never read** such an interesting book.
He will **hardly** know the answer.
She **nearly** bought that funny hat.

Only <u>I</u> spoke to him. (... nur <u>ich</u> ...)
I **only** <u>spoke</u> to him. (... ich <u>sprach</u> nur ...)
I spoke **only** <u>to him</u>. (... nur <u>mit ihm</u> ...)

– Manche **ursprüngliche Adverbien** steigern mit „very",
wenn nicht ein Vergleich ausgedrückt werden soll

Beachte!

Die Verneinung beim Komparativ wird meist mit „no"
oder „not ... any" gebildet.

Gebrauch des Adverbs:

– als **nähere Bestimmung** eines Verbs

– als **nähere Bestimmung** eines Adjektivs

– als **nähere Bestimmung** eines Adverbs

– als **nähere Bestimmung** eines Substantivs

Die Stellung des Adverbs:
... hängt ab von der Bedeutung des Adverbs für den Satzinhalt

– das **betonte Adverb** steht am Satzanfang oder Satzende

– das **unbetonte Adverb** steht **vor** dem Hauptverb; vor allem always, ever, never, often, sometimes, usually, soon, ...
ebenso: hardly, really, nearly, ...

– Adverbia wie „only", „very", ... stehen **vor** dem Wort, das sie näher bestimmen (wichtig für die Bedeutung des Satzes).

Is your coffee warm **enough**?
I bought a blouse and a skirt, **too**.
Do you want anything **else**?

Übung 74

He finished this letter **very quickly** (A) **this morning** (Z).
The twins were born **in London** (O) **in 1980** (Z).
He played the violine **well** (A) **at the concert** (O) **last night** (Z).

Übung 75

Beachte!

Grundsätzlich **nachgestellt** werden „enough", „too" (auch), „else" (sonst).

Beachte die Reihenfolge verschiedener Adverbien am Satzende:

Art und Weise (A) – Ort (O) – Zeit (Z)

Beachte den Gebrauch von Verben anstelle von Adverbien bei:

„angeblich", „anscheinend", „gerade", „hoffentlich", ...
(S. Bd. 1, S. 181 ff.)

ÜBUNGEN

70. Aus folgenden Eigenschaftswörtern sollen Umstandswörter gebildet werden!

slow, quick, careful, friendly, fast, sad, weekly, best, beautiful, daily, early, worse, ...

71. Der vollständige Satz soll auf Englisch wiedergegeben werden!

a) Joe was _____ boy in our class who failed the exam.
    (der einzige)

b) This accident happened ____ ten minutes ago.
    (erst)

c) What's the matter? The children are quite ____ today.
    (still)

d) When he returned Ann was _____ doing her exercises.
    (noch immer)

e) Mary is so pale today. – I'm afraid she isn't _____.
    (wohl, gut)

f) He did his work quite ____.
    (gut)

g) When Joe came back to the service station the mechanic was
   _____ repairing his car.
   (noch immer)

h) He got this letter ____ a minute ago.
    (erst)

i) How are you? – Quite ____, thanks.
    (gut)

j) On Christmas Eve the twins were _____ excited.
    (ziemlich)

72. Die Lücken sollen ergänzt werden!

① HARD–HARDLY:

a) Nelly's father ... works.

b) Sue's parents have to work ...

c) The Coopers ... ever go to seaside.

d) If Tom tries . . . , he'll finish his work in time.

e) Take your umbrella, it's raining . . .

② NEAR–NEARLY:

a) Joe was careless, so he . . . caused an accident.

b) Mrs Brown . . . bought that funny hat.

c) We live . . . the bus stop, that's why our flat is a bit noisy.

d) The children . . . failed the test.

e) The station is . . . the cathedral, you can't miss it.

③ LATE–LATELY:

a) Our friends haven't come to see us . . .

b) He was . . . , so he had to run.

c) As Pat had got up too . . . , he was . . . for school.

d) I happened to meet the Browns at the restaurant . . .

e) Don't be . . . again!

④ DEAR–DEARLY:

a) These pullovers sell . . .

b) He loves his fiancée . . .

c) He sold all his old cars . . .

d) Mum kissed Baby . . .

e) These handmade carpets sell . . .

⑤ FAIR–FAIRLY:

a) My friend is a . . . good skier.

b) The match Manchester : Newcastle was played . . .

c) Our doctor's secretary is a . . . good typist.

d) I won't ask him once again, he didn't behave . . .

e) English teams usually play . . .

6) CLOSE–CLOSELY:

a) The nurse held the baby ...
b) They have been ... connected ever since.
c) As she was afraid of being robbed, she held all her things ...
d) The Coopers and the Millers were ... connected, but that's long ago.
e) She hurried off holding her belongings ...

73. Es sollen Vergleiche nach folgendem Muster angestellt werden!

> write / careful: Ann, Pat, Nelly
>
> Ann writes carefully.
> Pat writes more carefully than Ann.
> Nelly writes most carefully.

a) speak French / good: Austrian children, Swiss children, French children
b) drive / fast: I, my friend, Niki Lauda
c) speak / distinct: I, my teacher, an actor
d) to be dressed / elegant: I, my friend, Princess Diana

74. Folgende Sätze sollen auf Englisch wiedergegeben werden!

a) Nur Tom wußte die Antwort.
b) Der Reporter interviewte nur den Minister.
c) Er sprach nur mit ihm.
d) Vater schreibt oft am Abend Briefe.
e) Sie macht ihre Arbeit immer am Abend.
f) Du brauchst sie nicht zu fragen, sie wird kaum die Antwort wissen.
g) Ich habe noch nie so ein interessantes Land gesehen.
h) Sie hätte beinahe diese teuren Ohrringe gekauft.
i) Ist deine Suppe warm genug?
j) Darf ich dir sonst noch etwas anbieten?
k) Nur ich kannte dieses Geheimnis.
l) Auf dieser Party sprach sie nur mit Tom.

75. *Folgende „Satzbausteine" sollen in die richtige Reihenfolge gebracht werden!*

a) [last night] [for the ball] [She] [elegantly] [dressed]

b) [He] [in Austria] [was born] [many years ago]

c) [carefully] [Joe] [did his work] [last week]

d) [her sausage] [Pussy] [immensely] [liked]

e) [very carefully] [last week] [did] [She] [her work]

f) [at the "White Horse"] [in a friendly way] [yesterday evening] [The waiter] [the meals] [served]

PREPOSITIONS

POSITION OF PREPOSITIONS

There is a book **on** the table
The children swam **across** the river.

What are you driving **at?**
What are you looking **for?**

The baby was well cared **for.**
The doctor was sent **for.**

The picture you are looking **at** was painted by Reynolds.

He took the book **from under** the desk.
They bought the picture **for about** 10 £.

They talked **about,** and laughed **at** her funny hat.

USE OF PARTICULAR PREPOSITIONS

Linz is situated **on** the Danube, **in** the sky, Shakespeare was born in Stratford-**on**-Avon, **on** the edge of the wood, to sit **at** one's desk, to knock **at** the door, to stop **at** the crossing, ...

to go **on** board, **on** shore, to go **to** a lake, **to** the seaside, ...

in the afternoon, **in** the evening, **on** Sundays, **on** a wet day, **on** the first of September, **at** night, **by** day, ...

DIE VORWÖRTER (PRÄPOSITIONEN)

1. DIE STELLUNG DER PRÄPOSITIONEN

Das **Vorwort** (die Präposition) steht im allgemeinen v o r dem Substantiv bzw. v o r dem Pronomen.

Die Präposition kann **nachgestellt** werden

– im Fragesatz

– im passiven Satz

– im Relativsatz

Beachte!

– mehrere Präpositionen können miteinander verknüpft werden

– unterschiedliche Präpositionen können ein gemeinsames Objekt haben

2. GEBRAUCH EINZELNER PRÄPOSITIONEN

AN / AM

– **mit Ortsangabe (WO?)**

in, on, at

– **mit Richtungsangabe (WOHIN?)**

on, to

– **mit Zeitangabe (WANN?)**

in, on, at, by

The teacher caught Bob **by** the arm.
Hundreds of people were running **past** the museum.

Übung 76

on earth, **on** the road, **in** the street, **in** the world, **in** town, **in** the country, **in** this picture, **at** the post office, **at** the airport, **at** the university, **at** the exhibition, ...

to the country, **to** the post office, **to** the bank, he sat down **on** the floor, **on** the grass, we lay down **in** the grass, **in** the field, ... the boat was floating **towards** the coast, ...

Übung 77

a letter **from** Australia, to come **from** abroad, ... the word "fiancé" comes **from** (the) French, ... to walk **out of,** to look **out of** the window, ...

- **andere Verwendung**
  by, past, (an ... vorbei)

Redewendungen:

an ... sterben	to die **of** ...
drei **an** der Zahl	three **in** number
an sich	**in** itself
an und für sich	properly speaking
es ist **an** dir, ...	it's **up** to you
denken **an** ...	to think **of** ...

AUF

- **mit Ortsangabe (WO?)**
  in, on, at

- **mit Richtungsangabe (WOHIN?)**
  to, on, in, towards (auf ... zu)

Redewendungen:

auf der Geige spielen	to play **on** the violin
auf Englisch	**in** English
auf seine Veranlassung	**on** his initiative
auf Lebenszeit	**for** life
auf ewig	**for** ever (and ever)
aufs höchste	**in** the highest degree
auf deine Verantwortung	**at** your risk
auf jeden Fall	**at** any rate, **by** all means
auf diese Weise	**in** this manner
auf Urlaub	**on** leave
auf der Hut sein	to be **on** one's guard

AUS

- **mit Richtungsangabe (WOHER?)**
  from, out of

She killed him **out of** jealousy.
He helped them **out of** pity.

This cup is made **of** plastic.
Steel is made **from** iron.

Übung 78

The Coopers live **out of** the town.
Tom and Joe met **outside** the cinema.

I'll show you some more interesting stamps **besides** this one.
There will be some more guests **besides** you.

There will be no boys there **except** you.
All the students passed the exam **except** Pat.

All **but** one came to the party.
He hardly eats anything **but** bananas.

Übung 79

- mit Angabe des Beweggrundes
  out of

Redewendungen:

... besteht **aus**, ist **aus** ... gemacht	made **of**
aus ... gemacht (Material wird verändert)	made **from**
aus diesem Grund	**for** this reason
aus Freude, Scherz	**for** joy, **for** fun
aus Unwissenheit	**from** ignorance
aus Versehen	**by** mistake

AUSSER

- **räumlich** (außerhalb)
  out of, outside

- **einschließend** (neben anderen)
  besides

- **ausschließend** (kein anderer, sonst niemand, sonst nichts)
  except, but („ausgenommen", nach: all, any, every)

Redewendungen:

außer Frage	**out of** the question
außer sich sein	to get **beside** oneself
außereuropäisch	**extra**-European
außergewöhnlich	**extra**ordinary

The zoo is **outside** the town.
They discussed the matter **out of doors**.

Übung 80

They live **near** the museum, Baden is **near** Vienna, ... the post office is **off** Oxford Street (in einer Seitengasse ...), to wait **at** the baker's, we are **at** the dinner, **at** table, ... he spent his holidays **with** his friends (= in their house), ... **by** the brook, **by** the fire, ...

by day, **on** my arrival, **on** his departure, **at** night, **at** sunrise, **at** sunset, **at** the ceremony, **at** his death, **at** first sight, ...

in good health, **in** fine weather, ...

Übung 81

We travelled from London **to** Reading.
Read **to** page 5.
Walk **as far as** the crossroads, then turn left.

AUSSEN

- „außerhalb": out, outside
- „im Freien": out of doors

Redewendungen:

außen und innen	**without** and **within**, **outside** and inside
Außenantenne	**outdoor** aerial
die Außenbezirke	the **outskirts**

BEI

- **mit Ortsangabe (WO?)**
  near, off, at, with, by

- **mit Zeitangabe (WANN?)**
  by, on, at
- **mit Angabe von Eigenschaften, Zuständen**

Redewendungen:

bei der Arbeit	**at** work
bei dieser Gelegenheit	**on** this occasion
bei mir	**with** me
bei der Hand	**at** hand
bei Gott	**by** God
bei weitem	**by** far

BIS

- **mit Ortsangabe**
  to, as far as, up to

How **far** are you walking with us?
Suddenly they found themselves in the water **up to** the knees.

We have school **till** three p. m.
Let's wait **until** 3.15.
... **from** eight **to** ten days ...
They lived in London **up to** 1960.
Our friends must be back **by** midnight.

The teacher asked the children to read **from** page 10 **to** page 15.
There were five **or** six cars in his garage.
As many as two hundred persons are expected.

Übung 82

He made a hole **through** the wall.
They watched the comet **through** the telescope.
They travelled **across** the United States.

Austria's most popular Emperor reigned **through** the latter half of the nineteenth century.
They all suffered terribly **throughout** the cold winter.

He sent the letter **by** post.
She got the job **by** influence, she got it **through** her friend.
I didn't like this novel: Mr Blacksmith was killed **by** poison.

Übung 83

The Red Indians were riding **towards** the camp.
The balcony of our house looks **towards** the sea.

- **mit Zeitangabe**
  till, until, from – to, up to
  by (bis spätestens)

- **mit Zahlenangabe**
  from – to, or, as many as (bis zu ...)

Redewendungen:
bis morgen   see you tomorrow
bis wohin?   how **far**?
bis ins kleinste   **down** to the smallest detail

DURCH

- **mit Ortsangabe**
  through, across (quer durch)

- **mit Zeitangabe**
  through, throughout (über einen Zeitraum)

- **mit Angabe des Mittels (WODURCH?)**
  by, through

Redewendung:
die ganze Nacht **durch**   all night long

GEGEN

- **mit Richtungsangabe**
  towards (auf ... zu)

They'll arrive **towards** evening.

Swimming back to our little island we had to fight **against** the waves.
The Celts fought **against** the Romans.
Don't lean **against** the wall!

Her attitude **towards** modern art is familiar to all of you.
His behaviour **towards** his best colleagues was disgraceful.
You know my aversion **to** vulgar words.

Übung 84

They are waiting for us **opposite** the station.
The Coopers' house is **opposite** the town hall.
Suddenly he found himself **face to face** with his enemy.

Übung 85

The children took their sledge and went **up** the hill.
They rowed their little boat **up** the river.

The little boat was floating **down** the Danube.

At the festival they all enjoyed themselves, **from** the headmaster **down to** the youngest pupil.

Übung 86

- mit (ungefährer) Zeitangabe
  towards

- Widerstand wird ausgedrückt
  against

- Gefühl, Haltung wird ausgedrückt
  towards, to

Redewendungen:

| Tabletten **gegen** ... | tablets **for** ... |
| gegen die Vernunft | **contrary** to reason |

GEGENÜBER

- mit Ortsangabe
  opposite, face to face (bei Personen)

HINAUF

- örtlich
  up

HINUNTER

- örtlich
  down

- im übertragenen Sinn
  from ... down (von ... hinunter bis)

The little cat hid **behind** the cupboard.
He was sitting **behind** me in the cinema.

Übung 87

In London, **in** New York, **in** Regent Street, **in** town, **in** the living-room, **in** church, **in** prison, **in** hospital, ...
at Newhill, **at** school, **at** the cinema, **at** the greengrocer's, **at** the bank, ... **on** the first floor, ... Have you ever been **to** Italy?

I'm going **to** town, **to** the cellar, we went **into** the shop, let's go **into** this cafeteria, the Danube flows **into** the Black Sea, ...

In the Middle Ages, **in** the 17th century, **in** winter, **in** summer, ... **in** the past, ... **at** the moment, **at** night, ...
He finished his exercises **within** a few minutes.

Übungen 88, 89

HINTER

– **örtlich**
behind

Redewendungen:

hinter etwas her sein	to be **after** something
das Schlimmste haben wir **hinter** uns	we're **out of** the woods now
hinter sich lassen	to leave **behind**

IN / IM

– **mit Ortsangabe (WO?)**
in (große Städte), at (kleine Städte)
on, to

– **mit Ortsangabe (WOHIN?)**
to, into

– **mit Zeitangabe (WANN?)**
in, at, within

Redewendungen:

einmal **im** Jahr	**once** a year
im Morgengrauen	**at** dawn
in einiger Entfernung	**at** a distance
in Verlegenheit	**at** a loss
im Dienst	**on** duty
im Gegenteil	**on** the contrary
im großen und ganzen	**on** the whole
in ärztlicher Behandlung	**under** medical treatment
in Reparatur	**under** repair
in meiner Macht	**within** my power
im Alter von	**at** the age of
in Reichweite	**within** reach
in der Regel	**as** a rule

The ambulance came **along** the street.
We sailed **along** the eastern coast of Sicily.

Come **with** me! Would you like to go to the theatre **with** me?
Mrs Brown came **in the company** of her daughter.

to go **by** bus, **by** tram, **by** car, ... to write **with** a fountain-pen (**in** ink), they got the bricks up to the fourth floor **by means of** pulley block, ...

Übung 90

after school, **after** supper, ...
It's ten minutes **past** six.

The dog ran **after** the children.
Will you travel **to** London?
He left **for** Cornwall, he went home (**nach** Hause).
The train **for** London leaves at 10.15.

According to the State Treaty ...
I sewed this dress **according to** the pattern.

LÄNGS/ENTLANG

- **örtlich**
  along

Redewendung:
Hier **entlang**, bitte!   This way, please!

MIT

- **in Begleitung (von)**
  with, in the company of
- **mit Angabe des Mittels (WODURCH?)**
  by, with, by means of

Redewendungen:

mit lauter (leiser) Stimme	**in** a loud (low) voice
mit einem Schlage	**at** a blow
mit 20 Jahren	**at** the age of 20
mit Gewalt	**by** force
mit Hilfe von	**by** means of

NACH

- **mit Zeitangabe**
  after, past (Uhr)
- **mit Zielangabe**
  after (hinter ... her), to, for

- **mit Angabe des Vorbildes, der Art und Weise**
  according to

Redewendungen:

nach unten ⎫ im Haus   **down**stairs
nach oben ⎭   **up**stairs

Übung 91

Mrs Brown lives **near** Cambridge.
His house is **near** the department store.

The sun is **near** setting.

I want to sit **beside** you.
Put the pots **beside** the pans.
We live **next to** the Coopers.
It was cold, so we sat **close by** the fire.

Besides gold, copper was mined in the Alps.

Übung 92

You can't draw **without** a pencil.
The robbers left the bank **without** the money.

They have been there **since** October.
The Coopers have been married **since** 1980.

They have been there **for** 10 months.
The Coopers have been married **for** 6 years.

Übung 93

einer **nach** dem anderen	one **by** one
meiner Meinung **nach**	**in** my opinion
nach meiner Uhr	**by** my watch
nach (gemäß) der Verschreibung	**up to** this prescription

NAHE

- **örtliche Bedeutung**
  near

- **zeitliche Bedeutung**
  near

NEBEN

- **örtlich (WO? WOHIN?)**
  beside, next to (unmittelbar neben), close by (dicht neben)

- **im übertragenen Sinn**
  besides (neben, „zusätzlich")

OHNE

- without

SEIT

- **der Beginn einer Handlung wird bezeichnet (SEIT WANN?)**
  since

- **die Dauer einer Handlung wird bezeichnet (WIE LANGE?)**
  for

Despite his efforts he couldn't win the race.
Joe couldn't pass the exam **in spite of** his excellent knowledge.

The dog jumped **over** the fence.
They put a blanket **over** the dead man.

The robins were flying **above** the trees.
"We are 3,000 ft. **above** sea-level", said the stewardess.
It's not so cold today, it's five degrees **above** zero.

The children swam **across** the river.
Their parents walked **across** the bridge.

Our friends stayed **over** Easter.
Did the Millers stay **over** night?

What do you know **about** Great Britain?
What did the teacher tell you **about** government and administration?
You've got to think **about** it.

Thorndike wrote books **on** psychology.
I wrote an essay **on** education.

We went to Sicily **via** Reggio.

Übung 94

TROTZ

– in spite of, despite

ÜBER

– **Bewegung, Ausbreitung wird ausgedrückt**
  over (mit und ohne Berührung)
– **in der Bedeutung „oberhalb von", „höher als"**
  above (ohne Berührung)
– **in der Bedeutung „quer über"**
  across
– **zeitlich**
  over (über einen Termin hinaus)
– **geistige Tätigkeit wird ausgedrückt**
  about
– **Titel von Aufsätzen, Büchern, ...**
  on
– **im übertragenen Sinn**
  via

Redewendungen:

über 100	more than a hundred
über meine Kräfte	beyond my strength
über 80 Jahre alt	past (over) 80 years ...
über kurz oder lang	sooner or later

The children swam **round (around)** the island.
The boy scouts sat **round** the fire.
Where are our three poodles? They must be somewhere **about** the house.

They arrived at **about** ten.

Übung 95

Our little cat likes to sit **under** Dad's desk.
They found shelter **under** an old oak-tree.

Looking down from the mountain we saw the village **below**.
Put on your fur-coat — it's 10 degrees **below** zero.
You shouldn't do that; it's **below (beneath)** your dignity.

He found a dandelion **among** the violets.

Übung 96

UM

- **mit Ortsangabe**
  round, around, (um ... herum), about (irgendwo herum)

- **mit Zeitangabe**
  about (ungefähr um)

Redewendungen:

um jeden Preis	**at** any price, **at** any rate
um einen hohen Preis	**at** a high price
um so besser	**all** the better

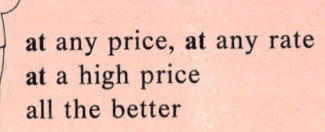

UNTER

- **mit Ortsangabe**
  under

- **in der Bedeutung „unterhalb"**
  below (ohne gegenseitige Berührung)
  below, beneath (unter der Würde)

- **in der Bedeutung „mitten unter" (einer Menge)**
  among

Redewendungen:

unter uns	**between** you and me
unter diesen Bedingungen	**under** these conditions
unter diesem Gesichtspunkt	**from** this point of view
was versteht man **unter** ...	what is meant **by** ...
unter 10 £	for less than 10 £

One of us should help him. Which of you will go there?
The town of Innsbruck, ... the month of June, ... a glass of water, a bottle of milk, ...
The Earl of Gloucester, the Duke of Edinburgh, ...

Rita comes from Italy.
The children are coming from school.
Little Tommy fell off his chair.
The actor walked off the stage.

We'll stop this smoking from tomorrow on.

An opera by Britten, a portrait by Reynolds, a comedy by Shaw, he did it by himself, ...

Übung 97

I met Tom in front of the cinema.
Suddenly the sea lay in front of us.

before Christ, before dinner, before World War I, ...
before ten o'clock, ... the day before yesterday, ...
I met him last two weeks ago.
A week ago it was sunny, ... a short time ago, ... years ago, ...

to tremble with fear, to die of influenza, to die of hunger, ...
to die from a wound, ... the houses are not safe from floods, ... they laughed for joy, ...

VON

- **allgemein** (Genitiv)
  of, bei Titeln vor Eigennamen

- **mit Richtungsangabe (WOHER?)**
  from, off (von ... herunter; weg)

- **mit Zeitangabe**
  from
- **mit Angabe des Urhebers**
  by

Redewendungen:

von Geburt	**by** birth
von Natur aus	**by** nature

VOR

- **mit Ortsangabe (WO?)**
  in front of
- **mit Zeitangabe**
  before (früher als), ago (von jetzt zurückgerechnet)

- **mit Angabe der Ursache**
  with, for, from, of

Übung 98

During the holidays they visited Cambridge.
Mr Brown was in Africa **during** the war.

The Coopers didn't come to Vienna **because of** the bad weather.
She got the job **on account** of her excellent knowledge and her good looks.

Übung 99

The children are **at** school ... **at** home, ... Joe sat **on** my right, Jim **on** my left, ...

we go **to** school, **to** the post office, we asked them **to** dinner, ...

at Christmas, **at** any time, **for** the first time, ...

it's **too** hot, **too** short, **too** long, ...

Redewendungen:

fünf Minuten **vor** zwölf	five minutes **to** twelve
vor allen Dingen	**above** all

WÄHREND

– during

WEGEN

– because of, on account of

Redewendungen:

von Amts **wegen**	officially
von Rechts **wegen**	**by** right

ZU

– **mit Ortsangabe (WO?)**
  at, on

– **mit Ortsangabe (WOHIN?)**
  to

– **mit Zeitangabe**
  at, for

– **vor Adjektiven und Adverbien**
  too **(ADVERB!)**

Übung 100

There's a little violet **among** the dandelions.
Share the sweets **among** you three.

She found the letter **between** the books.
Tom was sitting **between** two girls.

I can't remember exactly, but I think she returned **between** two and four.
All the work was done **between** five and six.

What's the difference **between** a mule and a horse?

Übung 101

Redewendungen:

zu Beginn	**at** the beginning
zu ebener Erde	**on** the ground-floor
zum Tal	downhill
zu verkaufen	**for** sale
zum Vergnügen	**for** pleasure
zu Fuß	**on** foot
zu Pferd	**on** horseback
zu Hunderten	**by** hundreds
zu Mittag	**at** noon
zum Gedächtnis von	**in** memory of
zu Mittag	**at** noon
zur Ehre von	**in** honour of
zu Besuch	**on** a visit

ZWISCHEN

– **in der Bedeutung** „unter mehreren", „in einer Menge"
  among

– **in der Bedeutung** „zwischen zweien", „in der Mitte"
  between

– **zeitliche Verwendung**
  between

– **andere Verwendung**
  the difference between

3. VERBEN MIT UNTERSCHIEDLICHEN PRÄPOSITIONEN

TO BE + PREPOSITIONS

to be back	zurück sein
to be around	irgendwo in unmittelbarer Umgebung sein
to be about	
to be out	nicht zu Hause sein, ausgegangen
to be out for	bemüht sein etwas zu bekommen; ... etwas zu gewinnen, ...
to be on	auf dem Programm stehen, stattfinden
to be over	vorbei sein
to be through with	fertig sein
to be off	weggehen, wegfahren, auf Reisen gehen, abgesagt sein, nicht stattfinden

TO BRING + PREPOSITIONS

to bring about	zustande bringen
to bring in	einführen, vorstellen
to bring round	wiederbeleben, wieder aufleben lassen
to bring up	aufziehen, erziehen (Kinder)

TO COME + PREPOSITIONS

to come across	(unerwartet) treffen
to come by	vorbeikommen
to come in	eintreten, hereinkommen
to come off	losgehen, stattfinden
to come around	wieder zu sich kommen, sich erholen, vorbeikommen, (nebenan) einen Besuch abstatten
to come upon	(unerwartet) entdecken

TO DO + PREPOSITIONS

to do away with	beseitigen, abschaffen
to do someone in	jemanden hineinlegen, umbringen
to do up	zurechtmachen, instandsetzen, renovieren
to do with	etwas unter Zuhilfenahme von ... tun
to do without	entbehren, ohne etwas auskommen

TO GET + PREPOSITIONS

to get at	erreichen, herankommen
to get down	aus-, absteigen, zu Papier bringen
to get on	besteigen, einsteigen
to get over	hinwegkommen über, herüberkommen, herübergelangen
to get on with someone	mit jemandem gut auskommen, sich gut verstehen

TO GIVE + PREPOSITIONS

to give away	verschenken, aufgeben, preisgeben
to give in	einreichen, anmelden, nachgeben
to give up	aufgeben, aufhören

TO MAKE + PREPOSITIONS

to make after	jemandem nachsetzen, verfolgen
to make off	weggehen, sich davonmachen, ausreißen
to make out	wahrnehmen, erkennen, entziffern

to make up	sich zurechtmachen, schminken
to make up to	schmeicheln, schöntun

TO LET + PREPOSITIONS

to let someone down	jemanden in Stich lassen, eine Vereinbarung brechen
to let off	abfeuern, abschießen, vom Stapel lassen
to let on	ein Geheimnis verraten, „plaudern"
to let up	nachlassen, aufhören

TO LOOK + PREPOSITIONS

to look after	aufpassen, sich kümmern, sorgen
to look at	anschauen, betrachten
to look for	suchen (nach), sich umsehen nach
to look forward to	sich freuen auf
to look on	zusehen, zuschauen
to look up	hinaufblicken; nachschauen, nachschlagen

TO PUT + PREPOSITIONS

to put into	übersetzen
to put off	weglegen, beiseite schieben, aufschieben
to put out	verwirren, aus der Fassung bringen, löschen
to put through	durchführen, ausführen; verbinden (Telefon)

TO SET + PREPOSITIONS

to set about	anfangen, beginnen, in Angriff nehmen
to set down	ansetzen, abstellen; schreiben
to set out	ausführlich darlegen, angeben; aufbrechen, sich aufmachen
to set on (upon)	über jemanden herfallen, angreifen
to set to	sich daran machen

TO TAKE + PREPOSITIONS

to take after	ähnlich sein, nach jemandem geraten
to take off	wegbringen; abheben (Flugzeug), ausziehen (Kleidung)
to take over	Verantwortung (Amt) übernehmen
to take to	sich einer Sache widmen, eine Gewohnheit entwickeln
to take up	aufnehmen, aufheben, sich für etwas interessieren, Tätigkeit aufnehmen

Übung 102

ÜBUNGEN

76. Die Präpositionen „AN/AM" sollen ergänzt werden!

a) Vienna is situated ... the Danube.
b) The teacher was sitting ... his desk, when the inspector entered the classroom.
c) Sue used to sleep ... day and to work ... night.
d) All the cars stopped ... the crossing.
e) All the passengers had to go ... board at 10.15.
f) The Coopers spent their holidays ... the seaside.
g) They arrived ... the evening – not ... noon.
h) He was born ... the first of September.
i) The policeman caught the thief ... the arm.

77. Die Präposition „AUF" soll ergänzt werden!

a) Naughty children. They always play ... the street, sometimes even ... the road.
b) The Millers will spend their holidays ... town – not ... the country.
c) She bought these special stamps ... the post office.
d) You'll get your tickets ... the airport.
e) They happened to meet old friends of theirs ... the university.
f) As there were no chairs, they sat down ... the floor.
g) George likes to play ... the violin.
h) What is „Auf Wiedersehen" ... English?
i) He decided to leave England ... ever.
j) The dockers will be on strike ... any rate.
k) Be ... your guard. He's a dangerous fellow.
l) I'll try it – ... your risk.

78. Folgende Sätze sollen auf Englisch wiedergegeben werden!

a) Gestern brachte der Briefträger eine Karte aus dem Ausland. – Ja, aus Schottland.
b) Sie schaute gerade aus dem Fenster, als der Unfall geschah.
c) Stahl wird aus Eisen hergestellt.
d) Dieser Pullover ist aus Wolle.
e) Er betrat diesen Raum aus Versehen.
f) Er sprach über dieses Geheimnis aus Unwissenheit.

79. *Der vollständige Satz soll auf Englisch wiedergegeben werden!*

a) Our friends live _____.
   (außerhalb des Dorfes)

b) I happened to meet one of my former teachers _____.
   (außerhalb der Schule)

c) There will be no girls _____.
   (außer dir)

d) There will be some more topics _____.
   (außer diesem hier)

e) All _____ took part in the conference.
   (außer einem)

f) She can't eat anything _____.
   (außer Porridge)

g) I can't come earlier, it's _____.
   (außer Frage)

h) The professor was so angry that he got _____.
   (außer sich)

i) Mister Jones wrote an _____ book.
   (außergewöhliches)

80. *Folgende Sätze sollen auf Englisch wiedergegeben werden!*

a) Heute ist es sonnig. Die Kinder können draußen (im Freien) spielen.
b) Heutzutage ziehen es viele Menschen vor, außerhalb der Stadt zu wohnen.
c) Ich glaube, wir könnten heute den Tee im Freien trinken.

81. *Der vollständige Satz soll auf Englisch wiedergegeben werden!*

a) Sitting _____ they had a splendid time.
   (beim Feuer)

b) We were _____ when an old friend of mine came to see us.
   (bei Tisch)

c) He spent his holidays _____.
   (bei seinen Großeltern)

d) Mrs Brown is _____.
   (bei guter Gesundheit)

e) _____ of the President many people had come to the airport.
   (Bei der Ankunft)

f) He recognized her _____.
   (beim ersten Anblick)

g) Have you got a knife _____?
   (bei der Hand)

h) _____ I'll tell her the truth.
   (Bei dieser Gelegenheit)

i) You can stay _____.
   (bei mir)

j) This book is _____ better than all the others.
   (bei weitem)

82. *Die Präposition „BIS" soll jeweils eingesetzt werden!*

a) The children have school ... 4 p.m.
b) The Millers lived in New York ... 1980.
c) You may go to the cinema, but I'd like you to be back ... 10.
d) The pupils had to read from page 10 ... page 20.
e) How ... did you walk?
f) She told me what had happened ... to the smallest detail.
g) Little Tommy found himself in the water ... to his nose.
h) I think you should wait ... 8.

83. *Folgende Sätze sollen auf Englisch wiedergegeben werden!*

a) Sag eurem Butler, er soll nicht durchs Schlüsselloch schauen.
b) Die Coopers fuhren quer durch Österreich.
c) Den ganzen Frühling hindurch war es sehr kalt.
d) Elizabeth I. regierte die zweite Hälfte des 16. Jahrhunderts hindurch.
e) Sie bekam die Anstellung durch Protektion.
f) Sie feierten Toms Geburtstag die ganze Nacht hindurch.

84. *Der vollständige Satz soll jeweils auf Englisch wiedergegeben werden!*

a) The windows of our flat _____.
   (schauen nach Osten)

b) All our guests will arrive _____.
   (gegen Mittag)

c) Every summer many tourists travel _____.
   (nach Süden)

d) Don't lean _____.
   (an die Tür)

e) The cats fought _____.
   (gegeneinander)

f) The Millers have always been polite _____
   _____. (ihren Nachbarn gegenüber)

85. *Folgende Sätze sollen auf Englisch wiedergegeben werden!*

a) Die Cooper-Zwillinge wohnen gegenüber der Schule.
b) Plötzlich standen sie einem Räuber gegenüber.
c) Die Kathedrale ist gegenüber dem Museum.

86. *Der vollständige Satz soll auf Englisch wiedergegeben werden!*

a) They put on their mountain boots and went _____
   _____. (den Hügel hinauf)

b) They rowed _____ with all their strength.
   (flußaufwärts)

c) Their houseboat was floating _____.
   (die Themse hinunter)

d) All the boys came running _____.
   (die Straße hinunter)

e) After dinner he went _____.
   (die Stiegen hinauf)

f) She came _____ like a queen.
   (die Stiegen herunter)

87. *Die Präposition „HINTER" soll jeweils ergänzt werden!*

a) Where is Pussy? She's ... the cupboard.
b) Tom sat ... me in class.
c) His hobby is collecting stamps. He's always ... some special stamps.
d) Are you ... some new dress?
e) She had been looking for her purse all day long. Suddenly she found it ... the cupboard.

88. *„IN" oder „IM" soll jeweils eingesetzt werden!*

a) The Coopers live ... Vienna.
b) They live ... the first floor.
c) Let's go ... this restaurant.
d) The Crusades took place ... the Middle Ages.

e) The Rhine flows ... the North Sea.
f) He finished his letter ... a few minutes.
g) Have you ever been ... France?
h) They saw the film ... the cinema – not ... TV.
i) He has all his money ... the bank.
j) All the children must go ... school.

89. Der vollständige Satz soll auf Englisch wiedergegeben werden!

a) When the professor asked him a question he was quite __ _____. (in Verlegenheit)

b) _____ they could watch some rabbits.
(In einiger Entfernung)

c) I can't give you a lift today, my car is _____.
(in Reparatur)

d) I think he's very greedy. – No, quite _____, he's rather generous. (im Gegenteil)

e) He has been _____ ever since.
(in ärztlicher Behandlung)

f) This policeman is _____.
(im Dienst)

g) He finished his studies _____ twenty-two.
(im Alter von)

90. Der vollständige Satz soll auf Englisch wiedergegeben werden!

a) She answered _____.
(mit leiser Stimme)

b) He won a million pounds – so he is rich now _____.
(mit einem Schlag)

c) The police had to open the door _____.
(mit Gewalt)

d) Our maths teacher always speaks _____.
(mit lauter Stimme)

e) They travel to Italy _____.
(mit der Bahn)

f) You should write _____, this letter must be written _____. (mit Füllfeder)
(mit Tinte)

g) Mrs Brown always takes her walk _____ .
(in Begleitung ihrer Tochter)

h) Would you like to go to the match _____? (mit mir)

91. Die Präposition „NACH" soll jeweils ergänzt werden!

a) It's 10 minutes ... four.
b) You may play in the park ... lunch.
c) I'd like to travel ... Scotland.
d) Last week Tom left ... Scotland.
e) The bus ... Manchester leaves at 10.30.
f) This medicine was prepared ... the doctor's prescription.
g) Your watch must be slow – ... my watch it's 10.15 already.
h) The dressmaker sewed this dress ... my pattern.

92. Folgende Sätze sollen auf Englisch wiedergegeben werden!

a) Joe möchte unmittelbar neben seinem Freund Jim sitzen.
b) Alle Kinder saßen dicht neben dem Lagerfeuer.
c) Stell das Wörterbuch neben das Lexikon.
d) Neben Psychologie studierte sie auch Philosophie.

93. Die Präposition „SEIT" soll eingesetzt werden!

a) The Smiths have been married ... 10 years.
They have been married ... 1977.

b) I haven't met him ... ages.
I haven't talked to him ... last winter.

c) The children have been learning English ... 1983.
They have been studying this language ... four years.

d) Joe has been writing letters ... two hours.
He has been writing letters ... 3 o'clock.

94. Die Präposition „ÜBER" soll eingesetzt werden!

a) Our dog quickly jumped ... the wall.
b) Where did you stay ... Christmas?
c) They went to Dover ... Calais.
d) Vienna is situated 260 metres ... sea-level.
e) It's 10 degrees ... zero.

f) What do you know ... London?
g) I can't carry this heavy box, that's ... my strength.
h) Did you read my last essay ... psychology?
i) It's really dangerous to walk ... this bridge.
j) The Millers travelled to Munich ... Salzburg.

95. *Die Präposition „UM" soll jeweils ergänzt werden!*

a) Where are the children? They must be somewhere ... the house.
b) She'll finish this work ... any price.
c) The boys sailed ... the island.
d) The guests arrived at the hotel at ... ten.
e) The full dress rehearsal will take place ... any rate.

96. *Der vollständige Satz soll auf Englisch wiedergegeben werden!*

a) It's rather cold today – 15 degrees _____.
   (unter Null)
b) Sue found a little golden ring _____.
   (unter den Blumen)
c) Where's Blacky? He's hiding _____.
   (unter dem Tisch)
d) This secret must remain _____.
   (unter uns)
e) _____ we can't accept this treaty.
   (Unter diesen Bedingungen)
f) _____ "balance of power"?
   (Was versteht man unter)
g) That's quite different _____.
   (unter diesem Gesichtspunkt)
h) This work is really _____.
   (unter deiner Würde)
i) Looking down from the plane we saw _____.
   (die kleinen Dörfer unterhalb)
j) You can buy any of these pullovers _____.
   (unter 10 £)

97. *Die Präposition „VON" soll jeweils ergänzt werden!*

a) Which ... you will go to the cinema today?
b) Madeleine comes ... France.

c) This drama was written ... Shakespeare.
d) Where are you coming ... ?
e) After the final curtain all the actors went ... the stage.
f) This portrait was painted ... Waldmüller.
g) I'd like another cup ... tea.
h) We'll stop smoking and drinking ... tomorrow on.

98. *Der vollständige Satz soll auf Englisch wiedergegeben werden!*

a) The children saw the film and trembled _____.
   (vor Angst)

b) I received your parcels _____.
   (vor zwei Wochen)

c) Come to lunch! It's _____.
   (fünf Minuten vor zwölf)

d) Julius Caesar was born _____.
   (vor Christus)

e) I'd like you to come _____.
   (vor dem Abendessen)

f) I happened to meet the Millers _____.
   (vor dem Museum)

g) The new guests arrived _____.
   (vorgestern)

h) I like musicals; _____ I like "My Fair Lady".
   (vor allem)

i) Our friends _____.
   (lachten aus voller Freude)

j) During the last war many soldiers died _____.
   (an ihren Wunden)

99. *Folgende Sätze sollen auf Englisch wiedergegeben werden!*

a) Wegen des schönen Wetters fahren jedes Jahr viele Leute nach Griechenland.

b) Wegen ihrer hervorragenden Sprachkenntnisse wurde sie als Sekretärin im Außenministerium angestellt.

c) Diese Schule war von Amts wegen geschlossen worden.

100. Der vollständige Satz soll auf Englisch wiedergegeben werden!

a) This house here is _____.
   (zu verkaufen)

b) This column was erected _____ Admiral Nelson.
   (zu Ehren von)

c) The spectators came _____.
   (zu Hunderten)

d) Don't you like to read books _____?
   (zum Vergnügen)

e) The Queen is _____ to Australia.
   (zu Besuch)

f) You should practise skiing slowly _____.
   (zu Beginn)

g) This skirt is really _____ for you.
   (zu lang)

h) If you look out of the window at 7.30, you may watch all the children go _____.
   (zur Schule)

i) You may come _____.
   (zu jeder beliebigen Zeit)

j) I was very delighted when I read this book _____.
   (zum ersten Mal)

k) Joe prefers to sit _____.
   (zu meiner Linken)

l) This memorial was erected _____ the brave soldiers.
   (zu Ehren)

101. Die Präposition „ZWISCHEN" soll jeweils eingesetzt werden!

a) Joe likes to sit ... two girls.
b) What's the difference ... a hen and a cock?
c) Share this bar of chocolate ... you four.
d) Sue found some lilies of the valley ... the violet.
e) I'll return ... 10.15 and 10.30.

102. Die richtige Präposition soll jeweils ergänzt werden!

a) about, out, on: I'd like to go to Covent Garden tonight – what's ... ?

b) up, round, in: Mrs Miller has brought ... five bright boys.

c) by, in, across: I was looking for my spectacles, but suddenly I came ... an interesting letter.

d) up, with, without: She can't do ... a cigarette.

e) on, down, at: That's a splendid idea — get it ...

f) away, up, in: His enemy was stronger than Joe, so he had to give ...

g) up, off, out: I can't make ... this sign; can you read it?

h) down, off, up: Be cautious! He'll let you ...

i) for, at, up: If you don't know the correct spelling, look it ... in your dictionary.

j) off, out, into: All his novels were put ... German.

k) on, to, out: When he came home, he set ... work immediately.

l) up, over, after: The Cooper children take ... their father.

THE NUMERALS

CARDINAL NUMBERS

1	one	21	twenty-one
2	two	22	twenty-two
3	three	23	twenty-three
4	four	24	twenty-four
5	five	25	twenty-five
6	six	26	twenty-six
7	seven	27	twenty-seven
8	eight	28	twenty-eight
9	nine	29	twenty-nine
10	ten	30	thirty
11	eleven	40	forty
12	twelve	50	fifty
13	thirteen	60	sixty
14	fourteen	70	seventy
15	fifteen	80	eighty
16	sixteen	90	ninety
17	seventeen	100	a (one) hundred
18	eighteen	1 000	a (one) thousand
19	nineteen	1 000 000	a (one) million
20	twenty	1 000 000 000	a thousand millions, a billion

twenty-three, thirty-four, forty-five, fifty-six ...

350 = three hundred **and** fifty
999 = nine hundred **and** ninety-nine

German: 45 379   English: 45,379
          2 328 170   2,328,170

Übung 103

DIE ZAHLWÖRTER (NUMERALE)

1. GRUNDZAHLEN (KARDINALZAHLEN)

„NULL" wird im Englischen auf verschiedene Arten wiedergegeben:

- **ZERO:** gibt den Nullpunkt einer Skala an: It's cold today, ten degrees below **zero**.

- **NOUGHT:** bezeichnet den Wert der Zahl „NULL" im Rechengebrauch: Three minus three leaves **nought**.

- **0 [əu]:** im gesprochenen Englisch, zur Angabe von Telefonnummern: 82 46 203 eight two four six two [əu] three

- **NIL:** zur Angabe von Spielresultaten: Manchester won the match 3 : 0 (three **nil**).

Beachte!

- Zehner und Einer werden durch einen **Bindestrich** verbunden

- Zwischen Zehner und Hunderter wird „AND" eingefügt

- Vor „hundert, tausend, eine Million" steht immer „a" oder „**one**", wenn es sich um **einhundert, eintausend, eine Million** handelt.

- Bei Zahlen mit mehr als drei Stellen steht nach jeder dritten Stelle vom Einer beginnend ein **Komma**.

German: 4,5   English: 4.5 (four **point** five)
0,82   0.82 (nought **point** eight two)

How much is this skirt, please? – It's £ 19.90 (nineteen pounds ninety)
How much are these socks, please? – They are $ 5.50 (five dollars fifty).

It's 10.15 (ten fifteen)   = It's a quarter past ten.
It's 10.30 (ten thirty)   = It's half past ten.
It's 10.45 (ten forty-five) = It's a quarter to eleven.

Joe was born in 1948 (nineteen forty eight) = nineteen hundred and forty eight.
This book was written in 1986 (nineteen eighty six) = nineteen hundred and eighty six.

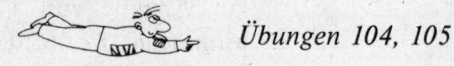

Übungen 104, 105

ORDINAL NUMBERS

1st	the first	21st	the twenty-first
2nd	the second	22nd	the twenty-second
3rd	the third	23rd	the twenty-third
4th	the fourth	24th	the twenty-fourth
5th	the fifth	25th	the twenty-fifth
6th	the sixth	26th	the twenty-sixth
7th	the seventh	27th	the twenty-seventh
8th	the eighth	28th	the twenty-eighth
9th	the ninth	29th	the twenty-ninth
10th	the tenth	30th	the thirtieth
11th	the eleventh	40th	the fortieth
12th	the twelfth	50th	the fiftieth
13th	the thirteenth	60th	the sixtieth
14th	the fourteenth	70th	the seventieth
15th	the fifteenth	80th	the eightieth
16th	the sixteenth	90th	the ninetieth
17th	the seventeenth	100th	the (one) hundredth
18th	the eighteenth	101st	the one hundred and first
19th	the nineteenth	225th	the two hundred and twenty-fifth
20th	the twentieth	1 000th	the (one) thousandth

Übung 106

- **Dezimalzahlen** erhalten einen **Dezimalpunkt**

- Angabe von Preisen

- Angabe der Uhrzeit

- Angabe von Jahreszahlen

2. ORDNUNGSZAHLEN (ORDINALZAHLEN)

Gebrauch:
- **Zur Angabe des Datums:**

    Tom was born on September 22nd, 1950.
or: Tom was born on 22nd September 1950.
    (... on the twenty-second of September.)

Beachte!

Das „th, nd ..." wird in Zeitungen und Geschäftsbriefen bei der Datumsangabe vielfach weggelassen.
Kurze Schreibweise: 22 / 9 / 50.

- **Zur genauen Bezeichnung von Herrschern:**

  James I   = James the First
  Elizabeth II = Elizabeth the Second

- **Kapitelüberschriften:**
  Chapter II = Second Chapter = Chapter Two

MULTIPLYING NUMBERS

Once upon a time there was an old witch ...

She read the text **twice** – then she could understand it.

Three times four make twelve.

He has won for the Austrian team more than a **hundred times.**

A single (ticket) to London, please.

Take the thread **double.**

Übung 107

FRACTIONAL NUMBERS, FUNDAMENTAL RULES OF ARITHMETIC

Share this cake: **one fifth** for Tom, **four fifth** for Fred, Jim, Joe, and Tim.
It will take you **a quarter** of an hour to translate this text.

$3 + 3 = 6$ ... three and three are six

$2 \times 3 = 6$ ... twice three are (make) six

$20 - 15 = 5$ ... twenty less fifteen are five

$20 : 4 = 5$ ... twenty divided by four make five

Übung 108

3. WIEDERHOLUNGS- UND VERVIELFÄLTIGUNGSZAHLEN

ein**mal**	once	vier**mal**	four times
zwei**mal**	twice	fünf**mal**	five times
drei**mal**	three times	hundert**mal**	a hundred times

ein**fach**	single
doppelt	double
drei**fach**	triple, threefold
vier**fach**	fourfold

4. BRUCHZAHLEN, GRUNDRECHNUNGSARTEN

$\frac{1}{2}$ = a (one) half

$\frac{1}{4}$ = a (one) fourth, a quarter

$\frac{3}{4}$ = three fourth, three quarters

$1\frac{1}{2}$ = one and a half

$3\frac{4}{5}$ = three and four fifth

- Addieren
- Multiplizieren
- Subtrahieren
- Dividieren

ÜBUNGEN

103. Folgende Zahlen sollen „in Worten" geschrieben werden!

a) 2, 12, 20
b) 3, 13, 30
c) 4, 14, 40
d) 5, 15, 50
e) 6, 16, 60
f) 7, 17, 70
g) 8, 18, 80
h) 9, 19, 90

104. Folgende Uhrzeiten sollen in Worten angegeben werden!

a) 3.02
b) 4.15
c) 5.25
d) 6.30
e) 7.32
f) 8.45
g) 9.50
h) 10.58

105. Die Jahreszahlen folgender Sätze sollen ausgeschrieben werden!

a) Guy Fawkes wanted to blow up the Houses of Parliament in London in 1605.
b) The Normans won the Battle of Hastings in 1066.
c) Admiral Nelson defeated Napoleon in the Battle of Trafalgar in 1805.
d) Rome was founded in 753 B. C.
e) Austria has been a republic since 1918.
f) The Austrian State Treaty was signed in 1955.

106. Folgende Daten sollen ausgeschrieben werden!

a) 1. Jänner 1987
b) 3. Februar 1950
c) 9. März 1964
d) 12. April 1970
e) 22. Mai 1975
f) 23. Juni 1980
g) 30. Juli 1982
h) 31. August 1984

107. Folgende Sätze sollen auf Englisch wiedergegeben werden!

a) Es war einmal ein Riese. Sein Name war Cucullin.
b) Sie muß zweimal pro Woche zum Zahnarzt gehen.
c) Sue ist schon zum vierten Mal in Rom.
d) Nimm den Faden dreifach.

108. Folgende Rechenoperationen sollen wiedergegeben werden!

a) $5 + 2 = 7$
b) $5 \times 2 = 10$
c) $15 - 5 = 10$
d) $15 : 5 = 3$

LÖSUNGEN

1. **a** man, **an** Englishman, **an** Italian, **a** university, **a** one-year-old-girl, **a** home, **a** Member of Parliament, **an** Austrian flag, **an** M.P., **a** house, **an** hour, **a** huge building, **an** ugly wizard, **an** American car, **a** red apple, **an** orange, **a** uniform, **an** interesting musical, **an** opera.

2. a) Tom wants to become a doctor.
   b) Only one boy of Fred's class became a mechanic.
   c) Is Mr Dupont a Frenchman? – No, he is an Italian.
   d) Look, Pat has disguised himself as a Red Indian.
   e) He was known as an excellent actor.
   f) She earned 120 £ a week.
   g) The curtains were sold at 3 £ a metre.
   h) The professor examined one at a time.
   i) The author will have finished this book in a week or two.
   j) Many a girl, who wants to become a secretary, becomes nothing but a typist.
   k) What a fashionable haircut you've got!
   l) Did you enjoy the film? Yes, it was quite an amusing film.
   m) Tom is much bigger, although Tom and his cousin are of an age.
   n) He'll be back in half an hour.
   o) A big stone served us as a table.

3. a) Mr Hoover was **a** Protestant. When he moved to Italy he turned Roman Catholic.
   b) Jim wants to become **a** teacher. His father is headmaster of Trinity College.
   c) All the people were in **a** hurry.
   d) The teacher spoke in **a** loud voice.
   e) Take **a** seat, please.
   f) Mr Brown was Captain of the "Sunflower".
   g) Now he is **a** mechanic.
   h) After working as **a** guide, she turned journalist.
   i) Mrs Brown was in **a** temper when Bob arrived late.
   j) I have **a** cough and **a** sore throat, and I'm sure I have **a** temperature, too.
   k) The student was quite at **a** loss ...
   l) He was elected Lord Mayor of London.

4.
	[ðə]	[ði]		[ðə]	[ði]
a)		×	f)		×
b)		×	g)	×	
c)	×		h)	×	
d)	×		i)		×
e)		×	j)		×

5. a) They crossed Austria from west to east.
   b) Carinthia lies in the south, Lower Austria in the north.
   c) They used to take a walk in the evening.
   d) It's impossible to earn double the money in half the time.
   e) Medieval Vienna is worth seeing.
   f) All the pupils of our college came to the party.
   g) All girls like dancing, all boys like eating.
   h) Not only the pupils but also the teachers took part in the play.
   i) They'll travel to Spain in spring.
   j) There were many temples in ancient Rome.
   k) Many Kings are buried in Westminster Abbey.
   l) Tower Bridge is a draw-bridge.
   m) American literature is known all over Europe.
   n) School starts in September.
   o) Heaven will help you.
   p) Most people go on holiday once a year.

6. a) ... from the beginning.
   b) ... in the presence of ...
   c) ... at first sight.
   d) ... at work.
   e) ... in practice.
   f) ... with the help of ...
   g) ... by bus.
   h) ... set sail.
   i) ... with the exception of ...
   j) ... it's the custom ...
   k) ... at hand ...
   l) In case of ...

7. a) Such is life.
   b) On **the** morning ...
   c) ... climbed **the** Dachstein and Ben Nevis.

d) ... quite at **a** loss.
e) It's **a** pity ...
f) School is over at two.
g) Fleet Street is the street of newspapers.
h) ... as **an** excellent scientist.
i) Mr Blackwell is **a** cashier ...
j) Mr Visconti is **an** Italian.
k) Old Mr Jones ...
l) Bregenz lies in the west.

8. a) woman g) queen l) drake
   b) master h) dog m) goose
   c) hostess i) daughter n) boy-friend
   d) duke j) father o) hen-robin
   e) heroine k) cow p) lion
   f) brother

9. a) ... and **his** peak.
   b) ... Scotland and **her** people.
   c) ... but **she** is still too young ...
   d) **She** brought the Pilgrim Fathers ...
   e) **She** is high up in the sky.
   f) **She's** landing on the new runway.
   g) Why is **he** barking again?
   h) **Her** fur is soft.
   i) ... is flying to **his** nest.
   j) ... the sun was shining in all **his** glory.

10. a) There are many boxes on the shelves.
    b) Many loaves of bread and many tomatoes are left.
    c) Tom's hobbies are rather expensive.
    d) Many gentlemen and many ladies were waiting at the bus stop.
    e) The children disguised themselves as wolves.
    f) Put these knives on the table.
    g) The farmer has many geese, many calves, and many oxen.
    h) Joe took many very interesting photos.

11. a) All his his **girl-friends** ...
    b) This play was written for the **ten-years-olds.**
    c) Leave all those **stay-at-homes** at home.

- d) She invited all her **sisters-in law** to her birthday party.
- e) The **lookers-on** applauded at the final curtain.
- f) Take two **spoonfuls** of milk.

12.
- a) Many thanks for your present.
- b) The dockers are on strike for higher wages.
- c) Many castles were built during the Middle Ages.
- d) The contents of this book are remarkable.
- e) The surroundings of Vienna are worth seeing.
- f) Where did you buy these tights?
- g) Hand me these binoculars, please.
- h) Yesterday I bought some new pyjamas.

13.
- a) The audience **is** applauding.
- b) Our family **dates** back ...
- c) ... the family **were** sitting round the fire.
- d) The police **wear** green uniforms.
- e) The crew of the "Atlantis" **are** very polite.
- f) A great number of spectators **were** expected.
- g) Plenty of time **was** wasted.
- h) A certain amount of diligence **is** necessary.

14.
- a) Before going to bed the children wash their hands and their faces.
- b) The children put on their anoraks and their caps.
- c) Eight persons lost their lives in this terrible accident.
- d) They were all shook up and lost their minds.

15.
- a) Tom's car
- b) my sisters' friends
- c) a glass of wine
- d) a bottle of beer
- e) the City of Vienna
- f) today's programme
- g) someone else's business
- h) today's newspaper

16.
- a) This is my house and that is **my parents'**.
- b) **St. Stephan's Church** is the most interesting church in Vienna.
- c) ... I think it's **Fred's car**.
- d) Tom likes Verdi's operas but he doesn't like **Wagner's operas**.
- e) She has been staying at **her friend's house**.
- f) ... but where did you put **Pat's**?

17. a) In this house she could sing and dance to her heart's content.
    b) Fred was at his wits' end when his car suddenly stopped.
    c) For pity's sake! What's the matter here?
    d) The twins have their birthday in the month of December.
    e) Joe was born in the State of Michigan.

18. a) Poor Blacky! Who'll care for him?
    b) She is an intelligent girl. – And how her parents boast of her!
    c) Don't make fun of them. They are poor.
    d) Did you write a picture postcard to him?
    e) This hat doesn't belong to me, it belongs to her.
    f) They gave the present to him, not to me.
    g) He sent me a parcel for my birthday.
    h) He promised them an outing to Salzburg.
    i) We sent them clothes, victuals, and toys.
    j) Whose are those bikes? They belong to us.
    k) Did the teacher lend you the book on Australia?
    l) Offer her the cake. She'll like it!

19. a) There are
    b) There is ...
    c) I'm sorry.
    d) I'm afraid so.
    e) I hope so.
    f) I'm glad ...
    g) I'm fine, ...
    h) She succeeded ...
    i) ... try.
    j) People say ...
    k) She is said ...
    l) The ambulance was sent for.

20. a) **It is he** who brought the letter.
    b) **It is they** who won the competition.
    c) **It is we** who are making such a noise.
    d) **It is she** who wrote that letter.

21. ... to you, it's yours.
    ... to him, it's his.
    ... to her, it's hers.
    ... to us, it's ours.
    ... to you, it's yours.
    ... to them, it's theirs.

22. a) Blow your nose and put on your pullover.
    b) What an accident! Tom broke his arm, Fred and Jack broke their legs.
    c) A headline: Twenty passengers lost their lives.
    d) He got into his car and off he went.
    e) He sat down and started with his work.
    f) Wash your hands before dinner.
    g) This girl has turned his head.
    h) It's very hot here, take off your coat.
    i) Put your hands out of your pockets when you speak to me.
    j) My head is aching.
    k) She ran her fingers through her hair and made up her mind.
    l) Give me your paw, Blacky!

23. a) Where did you hide **these books of mine?**
    b) **This new teacher of his** is very kind.
    c) Would you mind showing me **these photos of yours?**
    d) I'd like to see **this car of theirs.**
    e) **This house of theirs** was rather expensive.
    f) Joe went skating with **this three friends of his.**

24. a) You disguise yourself as a clown.
       He disguises himself as a clown.
       She disguises herself as a clown.
       We disguise ourselves as clowns.
       You disguise yourselves as clowns.
       They disguised themselves as clowns.

    b) You'll repair the car yourself.
       He'll repair the car himself.
       She'll repair the car herself.
       We'll repair the car ourselves.
       You'll repair the car yourselves.
       They'll repair the car themselves.

25. a) They were approaching the coast when they ran short of petrol.
    b) I'll tell you what had happened.
    c) Teachers and children are looking forward to the holidays.

d) Don't move.
e) They complained about the low wages.
f) I'm very tired, I want to lie down.
g) They happened to meet at the station.
h) They joined this party.

26. a) himself
    b) herself
    c) myself
    d) yourself
    e) ourselves

27. a) each other
    b) one another
    c) one another
    d) each other
    e) each other

28. a) These are my purses, those are your purses.
    b) These are your houses, those are their houses.
    c) These are John's pets, those are Nelly's pets.
    d) These are her rooms, those are John's rooms.

29. a) This morning it was extremely cold.
    b) In those days it was possible, in these days something like that would be impossible.
    c) The children want to improve their knowledge of English, that's why they go to Brighton every summer.
    d) He finished his studies this week.
    e) I think we can stop now. That'll do.

30. a) 1. When did the Coopers go skiing?
       2. Who went skiing?
       3. Where did the Coopers go skiing?
    b) 1. Who spent his holidays in Austria?
       2. Where did Tom spend his holidays?
       3. Why did Tom spend his holidays in Austria?
       4. What did he want to learn?
    c) 1. Who got to the theatre by bus?
       2. Where did Mary get to by bus?
       3. How did Mary get to the theatre?
       4. How long did it take Mary to get to the theatre?
    d) 1. When does Tom travel to New York?
       2. Who travels to New York?
       3. Where does Tom travel to?

- e) 1. Whose new hat is green?
  2. What is green?
  3. What colour is her new hat?
- f) 1. Who is sixteen years old?
  2. What age is Tom Smith?
- g) 1. Who bought a new car?
  2. What did Mr Cooper buy?
  3. How much did Mr Cooper pay for his new car?

31.
- a) How much
- b) Where
- c) What
- d) When
- e) How long
- f) Who
- g) How
- h) Which
- i) Which of
- j) Whose

32.
- a) What colour is your new pullover?
- b) What is "Grammatik" in English?
- c) What are these boxes here used for?
- d) What age is our president?
- e) What colour are your favourite shoes?

33.
- a) who
- b) who
- c) which
- d) which
- e) who
- f) whose
- g) whom
- h) to which
- i) whose
- j) whose
- k) which
- l) which

34.
- a) A shop-assistant is a person who sells goods in a shop or in a department store.
- b) A joiner is a person who makes tables, chairs, and cupboards ...
- c) A cook is a person who prepares meals.
- d) A hairdresser is a person who cuts and sets ladies' and men's hair.
- e) A playwright is a person who writes plays which are performed at a theatre.
- f) A gardener is a person who plants and waters flowers, bushes, and trees.

35.
- a) A screwdriver is a tool which is used for driving nails into the wall.
- b) A pair of scissors is used for cutting paper, clothes ...
- c) A knife is used for cutting bread, cakes ...

- d) A camera is a thing which is used for taking photos.
- e) A needle is a thing which is used for sewing dresses and suits.
- f) A typewriter is a thing which is used in offices to type business letters.

36.
- a) This is the finest meal **that I've ever eaten.**
- b) This is the best story **that I've ever read.**
- c) This is the most beautiful garden **that I've ever seen.**
- d) This is the farthest journey **that I've ever made.**
- e) This is the most helpful book **that I've ever found.**

37.
- a) At the clearence sales they bought everything that was cheap.
- b) The Bible was the only book that Mr Miller knew.
- c) The first Englishmen that settled in America were Puritans.
- d) He told me something that I can't forget.
- e) They told us things that were very interesting for us.
- f) This cardigan is just the colour that I've been looking for all the time.

38.
- a) Alcohol is a drug **many people can't do without.**
- b) What's the title of the story **Dad is looking for?**
- c) Where are all the photos **you wanted to show me?**
- d) What age is the woman **you were telling me about?**
- e) This is the mountain **I climbed last summer.**

39.
- a) –
- b) who
- c) –
- d) –
- e) who
- f) –
- g) that
- h) –
- i) which
- j) that
- k) who
- l) –

40. Lösungsvorschläge:
- a) This place reminds me of the time **when** I was young.
- b) This is the park **where** I used to play **when** I was a little girl.
- c) This is the reason **why** I don't like to study Russian.
- d) Friday is the day **when** the Coopers will arrive.
- e) Give me an explanation **why** you are late again.
- f) Here is the place **where** we had a picnic last year.
- g) And that was certainly not the reason **why** you are late again.

h) Let's fix the date **when** we shall meet next.
i) Find the place in your books **where** we stopped reading yesterday.
j) Little Tommy can't understand the reason **why** Dad didn't come home.

41. a) any ... any   c) some ... any ... some
    b) any ... some   d) some ... some

42. a) Is there anybody at the door?
    b) There must be someone at the door.
    c) Someone asked for you.
    d) It wasn't possible to find the key anywhere.
    e) I'm sure we'll find the key somewhere in the kitchen.
    f) Somehow we'll solve the problem. – I'm quite sure.
    g) "Is there anything else we can do for you?" asked the shop-assistant.
    h) If there is anything to be done, I can help you.

43. a) Every   e) any   i) Every
    b) Each   f) any   j) Every
    c) Each   g) Every k) Each
    d) any   h) Each   l) every

44. a) The friends meet every other day.
    b) Every now and then they went to the theatre.
    c) These pullovers are 10 £ each.
    d) Everything must be finished by midday.
    e) He was nearly everywhere.

45. a) All   c) All   e) whole
    b) whole d) All   f) whole

46. a) They went sightseeing all day long.
    b) On the whole it was quite an interesting film.
    c) They often quarrel, but they are friends after all.
    d) They were walking through the woods when – all of a sudden – a hunter appeared from behind the bushes.
    e) When they came out of the department store they had bought a whole lot of unnecessary things.

47. a) These two ladies are jealous.
    b) Both girls will travel to England in summer.
    c) Neither of the students will pass the exam.
    d) London is situated on either side of the Thames.
    e) Who will win the race, John or Fred? – I don't know, either may win.

48. a) The Millers live on the other side of the road.
    b) Joe and Fred played football, the others went cycling.
    c) Would you like another cup of tea?
    d) If this jacket doesn't fit, try another, please.
    e) Somebody else will show you the cathedral.
    f) They met at the restaurant the other day.
    g) I hope he'll finish his studies some time or other.
    h) I'd like to show you something else.

49. a) Don't ask anyone.
    b) None of her girl-friends came to her birthday party.
    c) I'm sure nobody will help you.
    d) Did you see anything? – No, nothing.
    e) That's top secret. – Don't tell anyone.

50. ① a) many   ② a) a few
    b) many   b) little
    c) much   c) a few
    d) Much   d) a little
    e) many   e) little ... a few

51. a) a lot of / plenty of
    b) several
    c) A large number of
    d) a lot of / a good deal of
    e) A great deal of

52. long – longer – longest
    happy – happier – happiest
    useful – more useful – most useful
    careful – more careful – most careful
    useless – more useless – most useless
    well – better – best
    bad – worse – worst

much – more – most
small – smaller – smallest
late – latter – last
far – further – furthest
far – farther – farthest
old – elder – eldest
old – older – oldest

53. a) The **nearest** post office ..., go to the **next** post office.
    ... **next** holidays?
    ... the **next** person ...
    b) ... the **latest** news?
    ... **last** summer ...
    ... **later** than I.
    ... the **latter** is my brother.
    ... the **latest** fashion ...
    c) ... **farther** ...
    ... for **further** news.
    ... no **further** help.
    d) ... **older** than ... his **elder** brother.
    ... the **oldest** picture ...
    ... the **eldest** member ...

54. a) Ben Nevis is high.
    The Großglockner is higher than Ben Nevis.
    The Kilimanjaro is highest.
    b) A scooter is fast.
    A car is faster than a scooter.
    An aeroplane is fastest.
    c) A pig is big.
    A bull is bigger than a pig.
    An elephant is biggest.
    d) Silver is expensive.
    Gold is more expensive than silver.
    Platinum is most expensive.
    e) Miss Austria is beautiful.
    Miss Europe is more beautiful than Miss Austria.
    Miss World is most beautiful.

55. a) bigger and bigger
    b) even more polite
    c) more and more interesting

d) higher and higher
e) very charming ... most intelligent
f) by far the most diligent
g) the greatest actor of all
h) more and more beautiful
i) far better
j) most remarkable
k) even more interesting
l) The more often ... the less

56. a) Tennis is my favourite sport. I like tennis best (most) of all.
b) Peter's elder brother returned from America. – He is two years older than Peter.
c) These mittens here are not made of wool. – Put on your woollen mittens.
d) Many children like wooden toys. This little toy train is made of wood.
e) This silk blouse was a bargain.
f) Many people admired her silken hair.

57. a) alike
b) alone
c) asleep
d) healthy
e) awake
f) Lonely
g) worth
h) calm
i) watchful
j) contented
k) still
l) content

58. **A Dutchman** speaks Dutch.
A Frenchman speaks French.
A Swiss speaks German, Italian and French.
A Chinese speaks Chinese.
An Englishman speaks English.
An Irishman speaks Irish.

59. a) The Austrian Alps are poor in gold and silver.
b) These words are characteristic of her bad manners.
c) This gothic cathedral is famous for its high steeple.
d) She was happy at his arrival.
e) This wine is typical of this region.
f) You should be kind to your neighbours.
g) Last February many children fell ill with the flu.

60. a) The murderer attacked his victims in broad daylight.
    b) You shouldn't tell this joke at school; it's a broad joke.
    c) By her broad accent we heard at once that she came from Manchester.
    d) A wide public came to see the exhibition.
    e) The wide world was to be admired at this exhibition.

61. ① a) clumsy   ② a) serious
    b) foolish   b) earnestly
    c) silly   c) grave
    d) dull   d) seriously
    e) stupid
    f) unwise

62. a) This firm has been in other hands ever since.
    b) Can you tell me the way to the town hall? – I'm a stranger here.
    c) She's too proud as to ask for outside help.
    d) I'm convinced she doesn't come from England; she has a foreign accent.

63. ① a) clever   ② a) great
    b) intelligent   b) large
    c) bright   c) big
    d) wise   d) tall
    e) sensible   e) grand
                          f) huge
                          g) big

64. a) A great many people came to see the exhibition.
    b) This singer is known for his big voice.
    c) She wanted us to mow the lawn; but that was a tall order.
    d) I'm sorry, I'm not much of a dancer.
    e) You should capitalize all these headlines.
    f) His death was a heavy loss.
    g) He made a big mistake, that's why he didn't get the job.
    h) In Austria the long vacations begin in July.

65. ① a) fine   ② a) short
    b) kind   b) smaller
    c) capable   c) little
    d) Right   d) minor
    e) good   e) short
    f) high / good   f) little
    g) steady
    h) Good

66. a) They left the court with a light heart.
    b) This cave is not easy of access.
    c) It's warm today. I'll put on my light coat.
    d) That's no easy job; these colours are highly inflammable.
    e) A gentle breeze was blowing and we could go surfing.

67. ① a) amusing   ② a) evil
    b) cheerful   b) bad
    c) gay   c) hard
    d) merry   d) base
    e) funny   e) wicked

68. a) Everything's in apple-pie order, many thanks.
    b) That's a fine excuse, a fine friend you are.
    c) One fine morning they met the Coopers.
    d) That's very kind of her, but I think these are only fair words.
    e) Lovely day today, isn't it?

69. ① a) beautiful ... good-looking/handsome   ② a) heavy
    b) nice   b) hard
    c) pretty   c) difficult
    d) fine   d) bad
    e) beautiful   e) dangerously

70. slowly, quickly, carefully, in a friendly way, fast, sadly, weekly, best, beautifully, daily, early, worse, . . .

71. a) the only   e) well   i) well
    b) only   f) well   j) pretty
    c) still   g) still
    d) still   h) only

72. ① a) hardly   ② a) nearly   ③ a) lately
        b) hard   b) nearly   b) late
        c) hardly   c) near   c) late ... late
        d) hard   d) nearly   d) lately
        e) hard   e) near   e) late

    ④ a) dear   ⑤ a) fairly   ⑥ a) close
        b) dearly   b) fair   b) closely
        c) dear   c) fairly   c) close
        d) dearly   d) fair   d) closely
        e) dear   e) fair   e) close

73. a) Austrian children speak French well.
       Swiss children speak French better than Austrian children.
       French children speak French best.
    b) I drive fast.
       My friend drives faster than I.
       Niki Lauda drives fastest.
    c) I speak distinctly.
       My teacher speaks more distinctly than I.
       An actor speaks most distinctly.
    d) I am dressed elegantly.
       My friend is dressed more elegantly than I.
       Princess Diana is dressed most elegantly.

74. a) Only Tom knew the answer.
    b) The reporter interviewed only the Minister.
    c) He spoke only to him.
    d) Dad often writes letters in the evening.
    e) She always does her work in the evening.
    f) It's no use asking her, she'll hardly know the answer.
    g) I've never seen such an interesting country.
    h) She nearly bought those expensive ear-rings.
    i) Is your soup warm enough?
    j) May I offer you something else?
    k) Only I knew this secret.
    l) At the party she spoke only to Tom.

75.
a) She dressed elegantly for the ball last night.
b) He was born in Austria many years ago.
c) Joe did his work carefully last week.
d) Pussy liked her sausage immensely.
e) She did her work very carefully last week.
f) The waiter served the meals in a friendly way at "The White Horse" yesterday evening.

76.
a) on
b) at
c) by ... at
d) at
e) on
f) at
g) in ... at
h) on
i) by

77.
a) in ... on
b) in ... in
c) at
d) at
e) at
f) on
g) on
h) in
i) for
j) at
k) on
l) At

78.
a) Yesterday the postman brought a letter from abroad. – Yes, from Scotland.
b) She was just looking out of the window, when the accident happened.
c) Steel is made from iron.
d) This pullover is made from wool.
e) He entered the room by mistake.
f) He talked about that secret from ignorance.

79.
a) out of the village.
b) outside the school.
c) except you.
d) besides this here.
e) but one
f) but porridge.
g) out of the question.
h) beside himself.
i) extraordinary

80.
a) It's sunny today, the children can play out of doors.
b) Nowadays many people prefer living outside the town.
c) I think we could heave our tea out of doors today.

81.
a) by the fire
b) at table
c) with his grandparents
d) in good health
e) On the arrival
f) at first sight
g) at hand?
h) On this occasion
i) with me.
j) by far

82. a) till   d) to   g) up
    b) up to   e) far   h) until
    c) by   f) down

83. a) Tell your butler not to look through the keyhole.
    b) The Coopers travelled across Austria.
    c) It was very cold throughout the whole spring.
    d) Elizabeth I reigned through the second half of the sixteenth century.
    e) She got the job by influence.
    f) They celebrated Tom's birthday all night long.

84. a) ... look towards the east.
    b) ... towards noon.
    c) ... towards the south.
    d) ... against the door.
    e) ... against one another.
    f) ... towards their neighbours.

85. a) The Cooper twins live opposite the school.
    b) Suddenly they found themselves face to face with a robber.
    c) The cathedral is opposite the museum.

86. a) ... up the hill.   d) ... down the street.
    b) ... up the river ...   e) ... upstairs.
    c) ... down the Thames.   f) ... downstairs...

87. a) behind   d) after
    b) behind   e) behind
    c) after

88. a) in   e) into   h) at ... on
    b) on   f) within   i) at
    c) into   g) to   j) to
    d) in

89. a) ... at a loss.
    b) At a distance ...
    c) ... under repair.
    d) ... on the contrary ...

e) ... under medical treatment ...
f) ... on duty.
g) ... at the age of ...

90. a) ... in a low voice.
b) ... at a blow.
c) ... by force.
d) ... in a loud voice.
e) ... by train.
f) ... with a fountain-pen, ... in ink.
g) ... in the company of her daughter.
h) ... with me?

91. a) past   e) for
    b) after   f) up to
    c) to   g) by
    d) for   h) according to

92. a) Joe wants to sit next to his friend Jim.
    b) All the children sat close by the campfire.
    c) Put the dictionary beside the encyclopedia.
    d) Besides psychology she studied philosophy.

93. a) for ... since   c) since ... for
    b) for ... since   d) for ... since

94. a) over   e) above   h) on
    b) over   f) about   i) across
    c) via   g) beyond   j) via
    d) above

95. a) about   d) about
    b) at   e) at
    c) around

96. a) ... below zero.
    b) ... among the flowers.
    c) ... under the table.
    d) ... between you and me.
    e) Under these conditions ...
    f) What is meant by ...
    g) ... from this point of view.
    h) ... beneath your dignity.

i) ... the little villages below.
j) ... for less than 10 £.

97. a) of   d) from   g) of
    b) from   e) off   h) from
    c) by   f) by

98. a) ... with fear.
    b) ... two weeks ago.
    c) ... five minutes to twelve.
    d) ... before Christ.
    e) ... before dinner.
    f) ... in front of the museum.
    g) ... the day before yesterday.
    h) ... above all ...
    i) ... laughed for joy.
    j) ... from their wounds.

99. a) Many people travel to Greece every year because of the fine weather.
    b) On account of her excellent knowledge of languages she was employed as a secretary in the Ministry of Foreign Affairs.
    c) This school had been closed officially.

100. a) ... for sale.   g) ... too long ...
     b) ... in honour of ...   h) ... to school.
     c) ... by hundreds.   i) ... at any time.
     d) ... for pleasure?   j) ... for the first time.
     e) ... on a visit ...   k) ... to my left.
     f) ... at the beginning.   l) ... in honour of ...

101. a) between   d) among
     b) between   e) between
     c) among

102. a) on   e) down   i) up
     b) up   f) in   j) into
     c) across   g) out   k) to
     d) without   h) down   l) after

103. a) two, twelve, twenty
  b) three, thirteen, thirty
  c) four, fourteen, forty
  d) five, fifteen, fifty
  e) six, sixteen, sixty
  f) seven, seventeen, seventy
  g) eight, eighteen, eighty
  h) nine, nineteen, ninety

104. a) Two minutes past three.
  b) A quarter past four.
  c) Twenty-five minutes past five.
  d) Half past six.
  e) Twenty-eight minutes to eight.
  f) A quarter to nine.
  g) Ten minutes to ten.
  h) Two minutes to eleven.

105. a) ... in sixteen five.
  b) ... in ten sixty-six.
  c) ... in eighteen five.
  d) ... seven hundred and fifty-three before Christ.
  e) ... since nineteen eighteen.
  f) ... in nineteen fifty-five.

106. a) The first of January nineteen eighty-seven.
  b) The third of February nineteen fifty.
  c) The ninth of March nineteen sixty-four.
  d) The twelfth of April nineteen seventy.
  e) The twenty-second of May nineteen seventy-five.
  f) The twenty-third of June nineteen eighty.
  g) The thirtieth of July nineteen eighty-two.
  h) The thirty-first of August nineteen eighty-four.

107. a) There was once a giant. His name was Cucullin.
  b) She must go to the dentist twice a week.
  c) Sue is in Rome for the fourth time.
  d) Take the thread threefold.

108. a) Five and two are seven.
  b) Five times two are (make) ten.
  c) Fifteen less five are ten.
  d) Fifteen divided by five make three.

STICHWORTVERZEICHNIS

A

about 181
above 179
across 179
Adjektiv 109
  Besonderheiten 111, 123, 125
  Steigerung und Anwendung 109
  mit Präpositionen 123
Adverb 149
  Bildung 149
  Steigerung 151
  Stellung 153
  Formgleichheit mit Adjektiv 149
after 175
against 171
ago 183
all 87
among 181, 187
an 161
another 91
any 83, 85, 87
Artikel 13
  bestimmter 19
  unbestimmter 13
  Stellung 15
at 185
auf 163
aus 163
außer 165

B

before 183
behind 173
bei 167
beneath 181
beside(s) 177
besitzanzeigendes Fürwort 63
bestimmter Artikel 19
  Aussprache 19
  Gebrauch 19
better/best 111
between 187
bezügliches Fürwort 79
bis 167
both 89
breit 125
Bruchzahl 207
by 175, 183

C

cardinal numbers 203
close(ly) 151
common case 47

D

Datum 205
deal, a great ... 95
definite article 19
demonstrative pronoun 71
Demonstrativpronomen 71
Dezimalzahl 205
dumm 125
durch 169
during 185

E

each (of) 85
each (other) 71
Eigenschaftswort 109
either 89
elder/eldest 113
else 155
emphatisches Pronomen 67
ernst 127
„es" 59
every 85

F

fair(ly) 151
farther/farthest 113
few 95
first 205
for 185
fractional numbers 207
Fragefürwort 75
fremd 127
from 183
further 113

G

gegen 169
gegenüber 171
Genus 31
  bei Personen 31
  bei Tieren 33
  bei Sachbezeich-
    nungen 33
gescheit 127
Geschlecht 31
groß 129
Grundrechnungsarten 207
Grundzahl 203
gut 131

H

hard(ly) 151
Hauptwort 31
hinauf 171
hinter 173
hinunter 171
hinweisendes Fürwort 71
how 77

I

-ics, Substantiv auf ... 41
„immer" +
  Komparativ 115
in 173
indefinite article 13
indefinite pronoun 85
interrogative pronoun 75
Interrogativpronomen 75
into 173
it 57, 59

J

Jahreszahlen 205

K

Kardinalzahlen 203
klein 133

L

längs 175
last 113
latter 113

least 111
leicht 135
less 111
little 95, 111
lot, a ... of 95
lustig 135
-ly (Adverb) 149

M

„man" 61
many 95
Mehrzahl 35, 37
mit 175
more 95, 111
most 95, 111
much 95
multiplying numbers 207

N

nach 175
nahe 177
near 177
neben 177
neither 89
nicht reflexiv gebrauchte
  Verben 69
no 91
nobody 91
none 91
nothing 91
noun 31
Numerale 203
Numerus 45

O

of 49, 183
off 183
ohne 177
on 179, 185
one 91
one ... another 71
only 153
ordinal numbers 205
Ordinalzahl 205
Ordnungszahl 205
other 91
out of 163
over 179

P

Personalpronomen 57
personal pronoun 57
plenty of 95
Plural 35, 37
  Formen 37
  von Fremdwörtern 39
possessive case 47
Possessivpronomen 63
preposition 161
Präposition 161
  Stellung 161
  Gebrauch 161
Pronomia 57

R

reflexive pronoun 67
Reflexivpronomen 67
relative pronoun 79
Relativpronomen 79
reziproke Pronomina 71
round 181

S

Satzgliederstellung 155
schlecht 135
schön 137
schwer 139
seit 177
„-self"-Pronomia 67
since 177
Singular 39, 43
some 83
some(body) 83
Steigerung des
  Adjektivs 109
Steigerung des
  Adverbs 151
Stellung
  des Adverbs 153
  des Artikels 15
Substantiv 31

T

that 79
that/those 73
the ... the 115
this/these 73
through(out) 169
too 155, 185
towards 169, 171
trotz 179
two, the ... 89

U

über 179
um 181
unbestimmter Artikel 13
  Form 13
  Aussprache 13
  Gebrauch 15
unbestimmtes Fürwort 83
under 181
unter 181

V

Vergleich 115
Vervielfältigungszahlen 207
von 183
vor 183

W

während 185
wegen 185
wer 79
what 77, 81
when 77, 81
where 77, 81
which 77, 79
whole 87
who(m) 79
whose 79
why 77, 81
Wiederholungszahl 207
worse/worst 111

Y

yours 65

Z

Zahlwort 203
zu 185
zwischen 185

NOTIZEN

NOTIZEN

NOTIZEN

NOTIZEN

NOTIZEN

NOTIZEN

NOTIZEN